DATE DUE

			PRINTED IN U.S.A.

BOOK OF SUCCESSFUL KITCHENS

H11D

BOOK OF SUCCESSFUL KITCHENS

by Patrick J. Galvin

STRUCTURES PUBLISHING COMPANY
Farmington, Michigan
1974

Manufactured in the United States of America.

Book designed by Richard Kinney.

Current Printing (last digit)
 10 9 8 7 6 5 4 3 2 1
International Standard Book Number: 0-912336-08-0
Library of Congress Catalog Card Number: 73-91024

Structures Publishing Company
Box 423, Farmington, Michigan 48024

Frontispiece Photo by Hedrich-Blessing, Chicago.
Jacket Photo by Julius Shulman, Los Angeles.

Color pictures on Page 16 reprinted from "House Beautiful", May, 1972.
Copyright, The Hearst Corporation, 1972.

Contents

Foreword

The kitchen is now the most important and expensive room in the house.

In the homes in which we over fifty folk were brought up, the kitchen was a necessary evil, closed off from the rest of the house. The only requirement for its location was proximity to the dining room, unless servants were involved, and then the kitchen could even be on another floor. The room had to be close to a rear or side door so that the "icebox" could be replenished by the messy "iceman who cometh" nearly every day. The kitchen was equipped by the builder with a sink and little else. Cabinets were frequently an item of furniture to be supplied by the occupant. The gas range was obviously an item to be moved when the family moved and you could have any color you wanted so long as it was stove black. The garbage disposer was a smelly pail under the sink which we had to carry out to the garbage can in the alley.

Today the kitchen is a thing of beauty, a joy to work in, and a proud possession. It is efficient, easy to clean, safe, well lit, sound conditioned, and well ventilated. Equipment includes one or more built-in ovens, ranges, refrigerators, a garbage disposal and lots of factory-built cabinetry styled to suit a variety of tastes. No longer is this room masked from the rest of the house, but other rooms are allied to it by open planning, folding doors and pass-throughs. The kitchen frequently accommodates table-type eating space or a snack bar. A wet bar, a cooled wine cellar, a trash compactor, menu planning desk, built-in mixing center, a communication center (intercom), and a color TV are increasingly incorporated.

When in 1972, we published the "Kitchen Planning Guide for Builders and Architects", we planned a not-so-technical book for homeowners and builders that would appeal to the group that purchases our "Book of Successful Fireplaces". Pat Galvin has again done a superb job of eliminating the technicalities in the larger book and adding material of a consumer interest. We believe that this book will answer your questions about Kitchens in an understandable, pleasant way.

For better Kitchens. . . .

R. J. Lytle, Publisher
Structures Publishing Co.

A kitchen with a country air, where the mellow fruitwood cabinets are styled with ageless Provincial detailing. The dishwasher, sinks and cooktop are along one wall and a preparation counter surfaced with a hardwood cutting board is convenient to both wall ovens and the refrigerator-freezer. Floor and backsplash are of mosaic tile. (American Olean Tile Co., photo)

Introduction

There is only one worthwhile gem of advice for the homeowner—or even the long-term apartment renter—who wants a new kitchen.

Don't fight the feeling!

There are many ways in this modern world to spend thousands of dollars. But consider—

—The European vacation is gone in two weeks, and so is the money.

—the second or third car is used up in three years, its value eroded and its currency spent.

—The fur coat is worn only a couple of dozen times per winter, and it wears out.

—The vacation home becomes a continuing expense and an increasing problem, little used for so big an investment.

—The mutual funds might grow, sure, but they might not.

—And so with other options.

A new kitchen is a totally different experience.

It's exciting and it's fun.

It is used continuously for long periods, for years.

It is used by everyone in the house.

But in being used, it isn't used up. It's permanent.

It makes the house more livable. It adds to the value of the house. It makes it more easily resold for a much higher price, or it makes the house worth keeping.

There is no way to lose in buying a new kitchen, *providing* it is done well and done right

To be done both well and right it must be done by experts, from the early planning stage through the tear-out of old cabinets and installation of everything new, to the final sweep-up of all the residues of hard work.

An expert is not necessarily your Uncle Jake—although it might be. An expert is not necessarily just anybody with a "Remodeling" sign on his pickup truck—although it might be. An expert is not necessarily an architect or a builder or a husband with a hammer—although it might be.

An expert *is* a professional with a verifiable expertise in the kitchen field. He is a space planner in this unique and specific specialty with knowledge of—literally—thousands of products that he can supply and install to make your kitchen more a success than it ever was before.

You might have many reasons for wanting a new kitchen.

It might be for any of the outstanding developments in kitchen design and equipment of the last ten years.

It might be because of the changing needs of a growing—or shrinking—family.

It might be because of your own changing social habits.

It might be to get the convenience, tailored to your own needs, that was not built into your old kitchen because it was not customized.

It might be simply for a new look.

Or a good enough reason is simply that you want it. And can afford it.

The options available to you; how to find an expert; how to work with him, and what to expect will be explained in Chapter 1.

And in the following chapters you will find, in detail, all the things you might want to know about all phases of kitchen design and kitchen equipment.

So go ahead, and don't fight the feeling.

Split cooktop, with two 2-burner units on either side of drop-in barbecue, adds a unique touch to this bright and airy kitchen. Ceiling windows brighten the room with daylight. (Hedrich-Blessing, photo)

Butcher-block top on island cooking center is increasingly popular both for utility and textural contrast. Bright blue plastic laminate of regular counters continues up backsplash area for ultimate in cleanability. Lighting for task areas is provided by recessed fixtures under wall cabinets, in this Wood-Mode kitchen.

Another Wood-Mode kitchen offers variety of textures with drainboard model stainless steel sink running into butcher block section, and cooking island covered with artificial brick veneer.

Shingled soffits and walls add interesting texture to this kitchen, which has carpeted floor and plastic laminate backsplash all the way to wall cabinets. (Wood-Mode photo)

Sheer elegance results from this wedding of wood and metal. Fully open to the living area, it becomes a showplace in the home. Sliding tambour doors in the island cooking-eating center, in the peninsula cleanup center and on the walls help retain the character of this kitchen. Island top is stainless steel to harmonize with brushed chrome of wall appliances—twin refrigerators on left, twin ovens on right. Island doubles as food preparation center, with refrigerators and sink equally handy. Circular vent hood is above. (Julius Shulman, photo) ⟶

Simple, compact kitchen packs individuality into small space through use of color and by staying open to adjacent dining area. Avocado woodgrain on cabinets and patterned wall covering are both plastic laminates by Formica.

The same kitchen from the dining side shows brunch space at counter, a more natural woodgrain backing the wall cabinets, and more use of matching plastic laminate on other interior walls.

Form rules this kitchen design with geometrics of ceiling above and highly-useful half-circle island below. Island does multiple duty as cooking center, phone center, brunch counter, tray and utensil storage center, and has maple top for cutting or chopping operations. High hood needs extra power.

Shelving takes the place of wall cabinets in this Western Hemlock kitchen by Edgar Wilson Smith, AIA, and shelving is fulling adjustable.

Artistry of Charles Cressent, 18th century French cabinet maker and sculptor, inspired this Country French cabinetry by Mutschler, and Cressent's combinations of wood and metal were emulated in kitchen design. Protruding countertop angles at sink add a design element, but also add work space.

Luminous ceiling adds most modern touch to kitchen in which Wood-Mode's Lexington cabinets and old-style wall covering suggest earlier era. Corner sink in far corner is for cleanup, near diswasher. Island sink with built-in mixer (near corner) makes this a food preparation center.

Provincial styling has a different look when created with darker, contrasting molding on light wood. Gold color tones throughout add an elegance to this kitchen. White on island top is glass ceramic inlay for cutting or for hot pans. (Wood-Mode photo)

Airy, pretty, gay, with muted greens and cheerful yellow, this kitchen has mobile serving cart with maple top, hides in the island when not in use. Island cook center has extra sink to provide water used in cooking or to serve as bar sink when work area in kitchen is busy, or for youngsters' drinks when they dash in from outdoors. (Wood-Mode photo)

Carpeted, single U-shaped kitchen with wall and base cabinets of peninsula opening on both sides. Impulse line by Del-Mar.

Interchangeable panel inserts in wall cabinets enable changes of mood in this Mutschler Mediterranean kitchen. The blue panels can be changed easily by the housewife for any other insert 1/8" thick. Arched entry, beamed ceiling extend the Mediterranean flavor.

Swiss Chalet is the style of this kitchen with pitched, beamed ceiling, brick walls and blue bottled glass inserts in cabinet doors. Special cabinet encloses countertop microwave oven in far corner. (Wood-Mode photo)

Indoor-outdoor kitchen has glass walls in backsplash area and above wall cabinets. Black and white cabinets are Del-Mar's Overture line. Red countertop matches red dishwasher and refrigerator.

Kitchen with everything has double wall oven, built-in refrigerator, food-warming drawer in cooking center island, barbecue alcove (red) in far wall, lots of glass to let the outdoors in. Here all yellow and red surfaces, including refrigerator front, are plastic laminate. (Formica photo)

Lighting is a major element in this kitchen, starting with the unusual octagonal cabinet overhanging dining area. Interior lighting accents fine crystal, under-cabinet light shines through amber bottled glass on dining area. Ceiling is fully luminous. (Wood-Mode photo)

An "Elbow-Room Kitchenette" is the name given this kitchen, designed by Western Wood Products Association in 6×14' of space. Appliance at left is Modern Maid's unique combination of eye-level oven, cooktop and dishwasher underneath. Cabinets are of Western Hemlock.

Strategic island adds needed counter space and storage in kitchen that otherwise might be too compact. Total built-in convenience includes double oven, cooktop, paper caddy behind sink and a true built-in refrigerator. Accessories above take the place of a soffit, and a skylight adds both natural light and visual appeal. (Hedrich-Blessing, photo)

Graceful blending of materials makes a showplace of this St. Charles steel kitchen, softened by pastel blue of the cabinets. Big wooden hood vents both barbecue and glass-ceramic cooktop to its right. Cooking center counters are topped with ceramic tile, but cleanup center (sink area) has plastic laminate. And softening it all, carpet underfoot.

Styled for family which loves antiques, this kitchen has soft-toned brick on floor and cooking wall, ceramic tile countertops all around, maple chopping-block island. Antique-styled lighting fixture is suspended from weathered beam. Cabinets are Colonial by Wood-Mode.

Steel cabinets by St. Charles hardly look like steel when they get Provincial moldings. This compact kitchen has everything, including good counter space. Backsplash and wall is ceramic tile, and paper caddy is built into wall. (Hedrich-Blessing, photo) ⟶

Complete entertainment center can be a stunning adjunct to the kitchen. This includes bar sink, under-counter refrigerator, and the small metal plate to right of sink is built-in mixing center. Fluorescent tubes under wall cabinets cast light down to work space, up through bottom of cabinets to illuminate glassware. Plastic laminate on counter simulates maple butcher block. (Mutschler photo)

This kitchen was designed to relate to the outdoors. It overlooks a lake at Chelsea, Mich. This adds meaning to the hand-split fieldstone on wall, brick floor, wood cathedral ceiling, century-old barnside paneling on pantry in far wall. (Wood-Mode photo)

Variations of brown integrate all elements of this kitchen, brightened by the pattern of backsplash and soffit. Counter lighting is recessed under wall cabinets, and a hydronic heating unit is almost hidden in kick space under sink. (Formica photo)

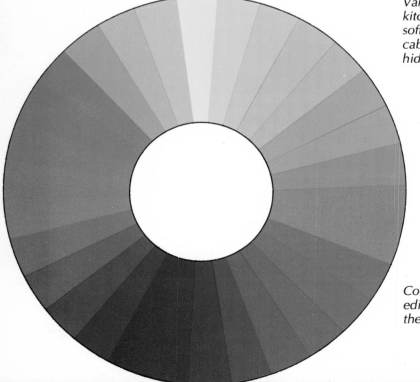

Color wheel from The Oxford Companion to Art, edited by Harold Osborne, 1970, by permission of the Clarendon Press, Oxford.

Carolina Oak kitchen by IXL (division of Westinghouse) gains added interest with peninsula and by carrying same wall covering through backsplash area and on soffit.

This kitchen, designed by Imperial Cabinet Co., forms a peninsula to provide both counter space and brunch area, then adds a brick peninsula to that for the Jenn-Air cooktop. Chandelier gives general light, supplemented by recessed down lights.

"His" area for hospitality is a feature of this modern kitchen by Rutt-Williams, with Georgetown style cabinets. Bar sink keeps hospitality function out of the way, and dining room cabinetry also supplied by Rutt-Williams is matching.

Even a one-wall kitchen can be distinctive. This one by Connor has pass-through at sink area to adjacent room and decorative opening over wall cabinets. And floor covering is duplicated on backsplash.

26

Modernistic kitchen at Horizon House, Lake Lindera, Cal., has eye appeal and total cleanability. Note the modern hanging lighting fixtures, supplemented by valance light at top of ventilating hood housing.

The warmth of redwood brings both elegance and a country flavor to this highly individual kitchen. augmented by good artificial lighting and a skylight that admits daylight. (Architect, Don Batchelder; Photo, Karl Riek; Courtesy California Redwood Association)

1

What's Do-able, and How to Do It

There are options open to you in remodeling your kitchen. You can take just a few steps, or you can take the whole trip. If the kitchen is more than ten years old, it might need a complete facelift. If it is less than ten years old some selective cosmetics might do the job for only a few hundred dollars.

Here are the options.

1. Partial remodeling. This might be to bring certain old appliances up to date, or it might be simply because you are tired of the appearance and want a new look. For this you can:
   a. Get new countertops. Plastic laminated countertops that have been built well and installed properly still look new after 20 years, unless they have been abused. But there are new colors, new textures, new patterns, and this is one product for the home that has gone down in price over the years.
   b. Resurface old cabinets. There are plastic laminated resurfacing products engineered to fit all of the old steel cabinets of the 1950s. These are sold nationally. In addition, kitchen dealers and plastic fabricators will perform this service in most areas on wood cabinets. But the cabinets must be in excellent condition or the resurfacing might not last. As a do-it-yourself activity you can do this yourself with some of the self-adhering roll materials on the market, or with vinyl wall coverings. But don't try unless you can make it perfect.
   c. Replace old appliances. You may have no idea what you're missing if your appliances were

supplied by a builder or if they are more than five or six years old. Read Chapter 4 before you decide.
   d. Other options. There are lesser measures that can have great effects. You can get new flooring (see Chapter 9), change wall or ceiling treatments (also Chapter 9), or, finally, bring the kitchen lighting up to the twentieth century (Chapter 7). Lighting alone can make a dramatic difference.
2. The full treatment. This means much more than replacing old equipment with new equipment.

It also means redesigning the entire kitchen so it can be worked in with fewer steps and less effort, less grouching and more smiling, so it is more functional for your family *the way it lives today.* The function of any kitchen changes when the family grows bigger or when it gets smaller, when the family income changes, when the family's social habits change, when tastes change (see Chapter 6).

So the first step is to make the decision. Will it be part way, or will it be all the way?

From that point on you have three options.

1. Will you—can you—do it yourself?
2. Should you let Uncle Jake do it?
3. Should you turn it over to a pro?

If you opt for doing it yourself—
—Are you really capable? Can you do the plumbing? The electrical work? The walls? The cabinet installation? Many decide they can handle the cabinet installation

and that they will call in pros for plumbing and electrical work. But read Chapter 3 before you decide. Remember, it must be perfect. If it looks like a home-handyman job the value of your house plunges, and if you ruin a cabinet there goes $40. Or more.

But if you insist on doing it yourself, at least have it designed by a professional kitchen specialist. It will cost a reasonable fee, but at least you won't be short-circuiting the dream before it starts.

If you opt for Uncle Jake—

—Or Cousin Charlie or Neighbor Nelson, fine, IF he happens to be a kitchen specialist or truly handy enough to do the job right. Otherwise, don't risk blowing your money or losing a friend or relative.

If you opt for a professional—

—You have chosen the wisest course. You are going to spend thousands of dollars, and with figures like that you've got to get your money's worth.

The next question becomes Which pro? How do you find him? There are firms everywhere that look like pros. How do you tell which are for real?

Here are the choices, and some groundrules to help guide you.

Home centers (or building supply dealers, or lumber yards)

These usually have displays of cabinets and appliances. You usually can buy everything, but often cannot get design service or installation. That's all right if you want the kitchen on that basis, but a design and installation service is strongly recommended.

Ask if they have a separate kitchen manager. Ask the manager if they design and install. Ask if he takes responsibility for plumbing and electrical work. Ask if he can give you names of satisfied customers. If all these answers are yes, you probably have a pro.

Department stores

They'll usually have appliance departments, might have cabinets. Like home centers, they must have separate, identifiable kitchen departments with separate managers and separate sales force.

Ask the same questions you ask at a home center. Often the good department stores will lease their kitchen departments to qualified kitchen specialists, and where this is true you have a pro. But if a salesman wanders over from the appliance or furniture department to sell you a kitchen, be wary. Such salesmen depend for their income on fast item sales and they can never afford the time-consuming consultation required for a proper kitchen sale.

Big national chains are included in this category. The big chains have some good kitchen departments, but they vary from city to city. Don't judge a store in your city by the performance of a similar store in another area.

Builders or architects

Unless they have separate divisions that specialize in remodeling, plus a track record in kitchens, forget them. Neither can afford this kind of work unless they are set up for it, and they won't know the products or the principles of kitchen design.

In recent years many small builders have turned to general remodeling, but in these cases look for a track record in kitchen work, or be sure they have added a kitchen specialist to the staff. Even very good builders are not necessarily good in kitchens.

Be sure, also, that your pro has a kitchen showroom where you can see a variety of kitchen equipment. A real pro will not expect you to spend that much money to buy out of a catalog.

Plumbing or electrical contractors

Some of these are among the best kitchen specialists in the country. But again, not necessarily. They must have separate, identifiable kitchen departments staffed by kitchen specialists and complete kitchen displays in their showrooms.

Appliance stores

Never, unless you find one with a separate kitchen department.

Yellow Page ads

Yes, there are "kitchen specialists" who exist only in the Yellow Pages. Be wary of ads that give phone numbers but no address, who offer everything from storm windows and siding to kitchens.

In Yellow Page ads look for evidence of a showroom, of years in business, of full responsibility for the entire job, of design and installation service, of professionalism.

Kitchen dealers

These are the people you want.

They have good showrooms with at least two complete kitchens on display, plus other partial displays. They'll usually have many photos of kitchens they have remodeled and they'll be glad to give you names and addresses of satisfied customers. They are permanent members of the community with an investment in the community. They must do your job professionally and well, because they depend for most of their business on word-of-mouth advertising.

These might be the kitchen departments of any of the businesses we already have mentioned. Or it might be a specialist who does only kitchens and baths, under names like "Kitchens by Jones" or "Kitchens, Inc."

When you walk in the door, you'll know you're in the right place.

The elite of kitchen dealers are members of the American Institute of Kitchen Dealers, and they will be listed separately in some 200 telephone directories across the U.S. There are about 1,000 members of this association, and they gain membership only by providing performance records and affidavits attesting to their professionalism.

And the elite of the elite will have the initials CKD after their names. CKDs are accredited by the American Institute of Kitchen Dealers as "Certified Kitchen Designers," and they might or might not be members of AIKD. But they always will have passed stringent and exacting tests to qualify as CKDs, and the CKD designation can be considered an equivalent of the AIA of the architect or the NSID of the interior decorator. A list of these appear in the back of the book.

What you should know about prices

Whether you go to Sears or Nationwide Home Center or Kitchens by Jones, you are going to pay essentially the same price for the same job. When you pay less, you will get less.

This is not like buying just a range or a cabinet or a new hat. When you buy items, you can shop for price.

But when you buy a kitchen you are buying professional services and skilled trades, and these are things that cannot be discounted.

Unless you want to live dangerously, you are buying from an established businessman who must pay taxes and wages and insurance and workman's comp and rent and countless other expenses that eat up 95 cents of every dollar he takes in.

The price paid for a professionally designed complete kitchen will probably run from 12 to 15 percent of the value of the home. These are just ball park figures. Consider it in terms of the kind of car you like to drive—you can buy anything from a Pinto to a Cadillac.

But remember, your car wears out in two or three years and you'll buy another one. Quite possibly you'll never buy another kitchen. So get the dream kitchen now, and pay for it. You'll be much better satisfied.

How the specialist designs your kitchen

Here's what to expect in buying a new kitchen.

1. You will visit the dealer's showroom.

Normally, he will demand this. He wants to escort you through the displays to see for himself what you like. He also wants you to realize his own investment in the community because it helps establish trust between you.

And he wants you to appreciate what the new products can do for you and what his design can do for you.

2. The salesman/designer will visit you in your home.

This is a necessary step to personalizing your new kitchen. He will want to discuss social and entertaining habits with you, observe your tastes in furnishings, observe structural details that will affect the job, and measure your kitchen himself. No good dealer ever trusts the customer's measurements. The husband and wife both must be at this meeting. You will discuss general price ranges.

3. You'll meet again for the presentation.

This probably will be in the showroom a few days later. The designer will have a proposed floorplan for your new kitchen, plus perspective drawings, color swatches, etc. At this meeting he'll want you to sign the contract, and you'll work together over the design to be sure it is tailored to your needs and desires, and to your price range.

He will give you a starting date and completion date. And he'll probably expect a down payment. Normally he will expect one third now, another third on delivery of the equipment, a final third on completion. He will help arrange financing if you need it.

4. Your next step is to wait.

The length of your wait will depend largely on the kind of cabinets you bought, stock or custom (see Chapter 3).

Custom cabinets are not made by the factory until your dealer sends the order in. Then they are made to order. This takes anywhere from six to twelve weeks, sometimes longer.

Stock cabinets are made in 3″ modules and usually are available to your dealer from a local distributor's warehouse. The dealer might even stock them himself. At any rate, installation can begin within a week if you select stock cabinets in standard sizes and if your dealer is not in a very busy period.

What to expect when the job starts

Kitchen modernization is a big job. It takes a lot of hard work. In making your kitchen great, there will be aspects that will grate on you.

The old cabinets must be torn out.

This means they must be cleared totally of all dishes and other things that might be in them.

And all those things must be put somewhere else.

And there will be a lot of dirt and debris.

There will be noise, and strangers in the house.

Water, gas and electricity must be turned off part of the time.

You will be denied use of your kitchen for a period of time which might be a couple of days or might be a couple of weeks.

All of this requires a lot of planning and a lot of patience, and a lot of putting-up-with.

Don't fight it. You are committed to it now, so make it easy on yourself and on the workmen.

Survival tips while the work's in progress

1. Be sure your kitchen is completely cleared of all dishes, utensils, foods, cleaning materials, any other items that might cause the workmen to stop and wonder what to do.
2. Dust gets around. There's no way to prevent it. So cover valuable fabrics and upholstery in adjacent rooms.

Another by Kitchens Unlimited features ceramic tile again on countertop, backsplash and floor, but appearance is quite different with free-standing range and white dishwasher. Appliances are Westinghouse. Base cabinet in corner is a pie-cut lazy susan.

3. Seal cracks around the interior doors with masking tape.

4. Plan meals out with friends, neighbors, relatives, anyone. Explain why, tell them they're invited to the "grand opening party" when the new kitchen is completed, and ask for help in your time of need.

5. Better yet, plan a vacation for this time.

6. While you are in the house and the kitchen is closed, remember you have water in the bathrooms and laundry. Buy or borrow an electric hotplate. Plan a few cookouts. If you are including a microwave oven in the new kitchen, get early delivery so you can use it now. Select foods for it (nearly all come with cookbooks).

7. Your dealer probably will give it to you anyway, but if he doesn't, ask for a complete schedule by time and date for when the water will be turned off, the gas, and the electricity. This way you will know what meals you must plan to eat with friends or from the outdoor grill. Confirm this with him by phone a day, at least, in advance of each such event.

8. Don't try to change the gameplan while work is in progress. The men working have no authority to make any changes.

9. Leave the workmen alone. Every time you try to talk with them you are slowing the job. Don't ask them to fix a bathroom faucet or put a shelf in the closet. The dealer is paying a man high wages to do the prescribed work, and your contracted priced depends on specific time factors for all of the labor.

10. Tell your designer-salesman you expect him to be there when the job is first started, to introduce you to the workmen. You don't want strangers out of nowhere.

11. Tell him also that you expect him there the minute the job is completed, so you can check it together. This way if anything is not quite right, it can be corrected while the workmen are still there. And it will prevent later hassles such as whether a countertop was chipped in installation or when you might have dropped a frying pan on it.

2

Basic Kitchen Measurements

The kitchen has no basic measurement standards that cannot be varied for cause. But unless there is cause, everything will work out better if the standardized measurements are followed. For example, the 84-inch total height of a kitchen installation from floor to top of wall cabinets squares off approximately with the top of the door trim, and it squares off precisely with the height of tall cabinets such as those used for broom storage, appliance enclosures, and pantries.

Basic Kitchen Dimensions. Here are the basic dimensions:

1) *Base cabinet*—height is 34-1/2 inches.
2) *Countertop*—1-1/2 inches thick.
3) *Backsplash attached to countertop*—4 inches high, minimum, can be 5 or 6 inches, or can extend upward all the way to the wall cabinets.
4) *Backsplash area from countertop to bottom of wall cabinets*—15 or 18 inches, depending on height of wall cabinets.
5) *Wall cabinets* are 30 or 33 inches high. The preferred height is 33 inches, but the most common is 30 inches.

All of these measurements combined will total 84 inches, from floor to the top of the wall cabinets.

Some multiple-housing builders, particularly in New York City, Chicago, scattered other cities, and the West Coast, have begun using 42-inch wall cabinets extending all the way to the ceiling. They claim they do this for esthetic reasons—for a cleaner look—and to gain added storage space in small kitchens.

It should be noted, however, that the minimum property standards do not accept storage space in the kitchen above the 74-inch line, and from a practical point of view such space is simply too hard to reach. Other standard kitchen dimensions are listed below:

1) *Wall cabinets*—12 inches deep, varying to 13 inches. Standard heights progress in 3-inch increments from 12 to 42 inches. Standard widths progress in 3-inch increments from 12 to 60 inches.
2) *Wall cabinets for general storage*—30 or 33 inches high.
3) *Wall cabinets over a range*—18 to 21 inches high.
4) *Wall cabinets over a refrigerator*—12 to 18 inches high, with 15 inches preferable.
5) *Wall cabinets over the sink*—if present these should be 21 to 27 inches high.
6) *Base cabinets* will be 24 to 24-1/2 inches deep, and will have a 4-inch kick-space. Height will be 34-1/2 inches, and widths will vary in 3-inch increments from 9 to 60 inches.
7) *Base cabinets used for kitchen desks or for buffets*—28-1/2 inches high. Units used for bathroom vanities are 30 inches high.
8) *Tall utility cabinets (84 inches)*—usually 24 or 24-1/2 inches deep, although some are half-sized at 12 inches or more. Width ranges from 12 to 42 inches in 3-inch increments. These come in variable configurations. Some have space for upright broom storage in addition to open shelving and/or drawers. Those used for pantries might have a series of revolving shelves or vertical shelving systems that fold out into the room.

Minimum Property Standards

HUD Minimum Property Standards. The Minimum Property Standards of the U.S. Department of Housing and Urban Development furnish a starting point in kitchen space planning, because these standards must be met or exceeded in any housing units where federally insured mortgages are involved.

Through 1971–1973 these standards were totally rewritten (for the first time since 1956), and builders and architects will probably find the new standards much easier to work with. As a whole, they recognize more fully the environmental factors in the home and in the urban area, are oriented more toward performance, and tend to encourage design innovations and improved building technologies.

Following are all requirements pertinent to kitchens in one- and two-family houses.

Kitchen Cabinet Requirements

| Work Centers | Minimum Frontage | | |
	Two Bedrooms	Three Bedrooms	Four or More Bedrooms
Sink	24"	32"	32"
counter and base cab. at each side	20"	24"	30"
Range	24"	30"	30"
counter and base cab. at one side	20"	24"	30"
Refrigerator (space)	36"	36"	36"
counter at latch side	15"	15"	18"
Mixing (base and wall cabinet)	36"	36"	42"

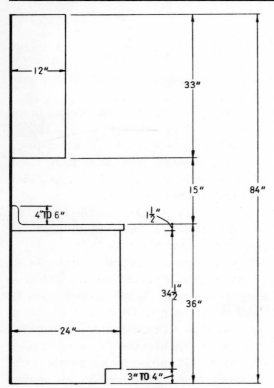

Basic measurements for kitchen cabinets.

Dining area minimums

Space for accommodating the following size table and chairs with proper circulation space in the dining area shall be provided, according to the intended occupancy, as shown:

(2 bedrooms)	4 persons	-2'6"×3'2"
(3 bedrooms)	6 persons	-3'4"×4'0" or 4'0"round
(4 bedrooms)	8 persons	-3'4"×6'0" or 4'0"×4'0"
(5 bedrooms)	10 persons	-3'4"×8'0" or 4'0"×6'0"
(6 bedrooms)	12 persons	-4'0"×8'0"
Dining chairs		-1'6"×1'6"

Kitchen specifications

The kitchen design shall provide for efficient food and utensil storage, and serving, as well as cleaning up after meals.

The kitchen shall be directly accessible to the dining area and shall be conveniently located near the living area.

Circulation space in food preparation areas shall not be less than 40" in width.

1) Work centers may be combined; the kitchen multiple-use space shall at least equal the largest frontage of any one of the work centers being combined, plus 6 inches.
2) Provide a drawer at each base cabinet, or equivalent group of drawers.
3) Frontage may continue around a corner, except a space less than 12" may not be counted.
4) Frontage of wall cabinets shall equal the required frontage for base cabinets.
5) The frontages are based on typical cabinets. Base cabinet approximately 24 inches deep by 36 inches in height with one shelf and drawer. Wall cabinet approximately 12 inches deep by 30 inches in height with two shelves.
6) Provide at least 9 inches from the edge of the sink or range to any adjacent corner cabinet, and 16 inches from the latch side of the refrigerator

Specifications page by the National Kitchen Cabinet Association shows typical wall, base, and tall cabinets with their customary sizes as made by most stock cabinet manufacturers.

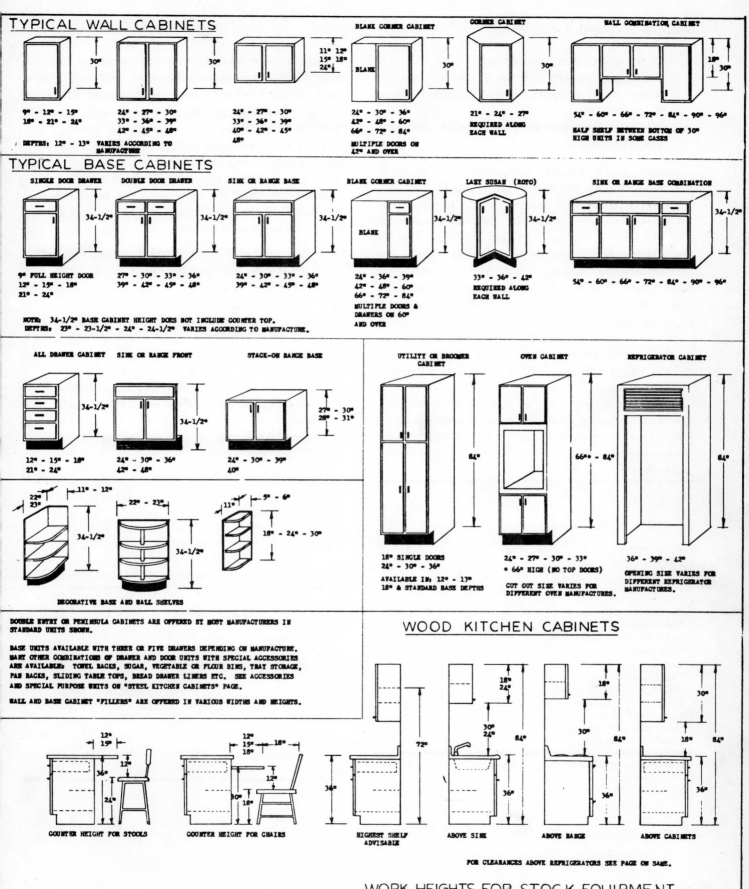

TYPICAL WALL CABINETS

BLANK CORNER CABINET

11" 12"
15" 18"
24"

30"

30"

30"

BLANK

30"

CORNER CABINET

30"

WALL COMBINATION CABINET

18"
30"

9" - 12" - 15"
18" - 21" - 24"

DEPTHS: 12" - 13" VARIES ACCORDING TO
MANUFACTURE

24" - 27" - 30"
33" - 36" - 39"
42" - 45" - 48"

24" - 27" - 30"
33" - 36" - 39"
40" - 42" - 45"
48"

24" - 30" - 36"
42" - 48" - 60"
66" - 72" - 84"

MULTIPLE DOORS ON
42" AND OVER

21" - 24" - 27"

REQUIRED ALONG
EACH WALL

54" - 60" - 66" - 72" - 84" - 90" - 96"

HALF SHELF BETWEEN BOTTOM OF 30"
HIGH UNITS IN SOME CASES

TYPICAL BASE CABINETS

SINGLE DOOR DRAWER — 34-1/2"

DOUBLE DOOR DRAWER — 34-1/2"

SINK OR RANGE BASE — 34-1/2"

BLANK CORNER CABINET — 34-1/2"

BLANK

LAZY SUSAN (ROTO) — 34-1/2"

SINK OR RANGE BASE COMBINATION — 34-1/2"

9" FULL HEIGHT DOOR
12" - 15" - 18"
21" - 24"

27" - 30" - 33" - 36"
39" - 42" - 45" - 48"

24" - 30" - 33" - 36"
39" - 42" - 45" - 48"

24" - 36" - 39"
42" - 48" - 60"
66" - 72" - 84"

MULTIPLE DOORS &
DRAWERS ON 60"
AND OVER

33" - 36" - 42"

REQUIRED ALONG
EACH WALL

54" - 60" - 66" - 72" - 84" - 90" - 96"

NOTE: 34-1/2" BASE CABINET HEIGHT DOES NOT INCLUDE COUNTER TOP.
DEPTHS: 23" - 23-1/2" - 24" - 24-1/2" VARIES ACCORDING TO MANUFACTURE.

ALL DRAWER CABINET — 34-1/2"

SINK OR RANGE FRONT — 34-1/2"

STACK-ON RANGE BASE — 27" - 30" / 28" - 31"

12" - 15" - 18"
21" - 24"

24" - 30" - 36"
42" - 48"

24" - 30" - 39"
40"

UTILITY OR BROOM CABINET — 84"

OVEN CABINET — 66" - 84"

REFRIGERATOR CABINET — 84"

18" SINGLE DOORS
24" - 30" - 36"

AVAILABLE IN: 12" - 13"
18" & STANDARD BASE DEPTHS

24" - 27" - 30" - 33"
* 66" HIGH (NO TOP DOORS)

CUT OUT SIZE VARIES FOR
DIFFERENT OVEN MANUFACTURES.

36" - 39" - 42"

OPENING SIZE VARIES FOR
DIFFERENT REFRIGERATOR
MANUFACTURES.

22"
23"

11" - 12"

34-1/2"

22" - 23"

34-1/2"

11"

5" - 6"

18" - 24" - 30"

DECORATIVE BASE AND WALL SHELVES

DOUBLE ENTRY OR PENINSULA CABINETS ARE OFFERED BY MOST MANUFACTURERS IN
STANDARD UNITS SHOWN.

BASE UNITS AVAILABLE WITH THREE OR FIVE DRAWERS DEPENDING ON MANUFACTURE.
MANY OTHER COMBINATIONS OF DRAWER AND DOOR UNITS WITH SPECIAL ACCESSORIES
ARE AVAILABLE: TOWEL RACKS, SUGAR, VEGETABLE OR FLOUR BINS, TRAY STORAGE,
PAN RACKS, SLIDING TABLE TOPS, BREAD DRAWER LINERS ETC. SEE ACCESSORIES
AND SPECIAL PURPOSE UNITS ON "STEEL KITCHEN CABINETS" PAGE.

WALL AND BASE CABINET "FILLERS" ARE OFFERED IN VARIOUS WIDTHS AND HEIGHTS.

WOOD KITCHEN CABINETS

12"
15"

12"

36"

24"

COUNTER HEIGHT FOR STOOLS

12"
15"
18"

18"

12"

30"

18"

COUNTER HEIGHT FOR CHAIRS

72"

36"

**HIGHEST SHELF
ADVISABLE**

18"
24"

30"
24"

84"

36"

ABOVE SINK

18"

30"

84"

36"

ABOVE RANGE

30"

18"

84"

36"

ABOVE CABINETS

FOR CLEARANCES ABOVE REFRIGERATORS SEE PAGE ON SAME.

IDEAL WORK HEIGHTS   SCALE: 1/4" = 1' - 0"

WORK HEIGHTS FOR STOCK EQUIPMENT
AND IDEAL CLEARANCES ABOVE COUNTER

to any adjacent corner cabinet.

7) Refrigerator space may be 33 inches when a refrigerator is provided and the door opens within its own width.

8) Where dishwashers are provided, 24-inch sinks are acceptable.

Recommended Kitchen Measurements. The HUD Minimum Property Standards are workable, and they represent a tremendous improvement over those used for the previous 15 years. But they are minimums, and even for dwellings intended for small families the prudent builder would do well to expand the countertop and cabinet capacities. And since they leave more open to interpretation than the old standards, it is possible to make them even more minimal. For example, by combining work areas it would be possible to get off with as little as 52 inches of lineal counter space in a two-bedroom house. But in this instance a little added cost can add a great deal of appeal and usefulness.

The countertop is for the purpose of serving the sink and appliances, and thus basic countertop needs do not change greatly as the size of the family increases.

Table 2.4.

Electrical Equipment Demand	
	Diversified demand (KW)
Basic demand	4.0
Clothes washer	.8
Dishwasher	1.2
Range	12.
Oven, built-in	4.5
Top, built-in (4 units)	6.0
Clothes dryer:	5.0
Water heater: (high recovery)	5.5
Food freezer	.6
Food waste disposer	.4
Water pump	.4
Attic fan	.4
Electric bathroom heater (each)	1.3
Central heating system (1)	.5
Room air conditioner (each)	1.2
Central air conditioner (1)	(2)

(1) Only the larger of the heating or cooling load need be considered.
(2) Rated wattage.

Basic cabinet requirements do change as the size of the family increases because of the need for increased food storage and the necessity of storing additional dishes. Other requirements, such as storage for utensils and small appliances, remain largely the same.

The HUD minimums (by the wildest possible interpretation) are compared with other figures more in line with what a kitchen expert might recommend.

In augumenting the minimums for larger kitchens for larger houses and larger families, there are the following recommendations:

1) *Dry vegetable storage* is best accommodated by a 3-drawer base cabinet (no shelves).

2) *Bread and cake* storage is best accommodated by a 3-drawer base cabinet.

3) *Sink area* (within easy reach of sink) is best accommodated by a 2-drawer base cabinet (which will have one shelf). This augments the storage provided by the floor of the sink cabinet.

4) *General storage* is adequately accommodated by 1-drawer 2-shelf base cabinets. This includes pots and pans.

5) *Small appliance storage* is best accommodated by pull-out shelves.

For basic needs and measurements in the distribution of countertop space and for kitchen brunch and dining areas, see Chapter 6.

MEASUREMENTS: MINIMUM VS. RECOMMENDED

	Counter (Lineal)	Base Cabinets (Lineal)	Wall Cabinets (Lineal)
1 or 2 bedrooms			
(HUD minimums)	52"	68"	68"
(Generous)	84"	96"	96"
3 bedrooms			
(HUD minimums)	60"	72"	72"
(Generous)	96"	120"	144"
4 bedrooms			
(HUD minimums)	72"	84"	84"
(Generous)	108"	120"	168"

3

Everything You Should Know about Kitchen Cabinets

Kitchen cabinets come in an almost endless variety of sizes, shapes, styles, finishes, colors and materials. This helps make them very adaptable as built-in furniture in other rooms of the house—such as rec rooms, bedrooms, music/education rooms, libraries—and homeowners should ask their kitchen designers about this.

But two classifications to be aware of are stock and custom cabinets.

Stock cabinets are manufactured in 3-inch modules and are stocked in volume in local or regional warehouses. This means they are quickly available, usually within a few days.

Custom cabinets are not built by the factory until the local customer has signed a contract for a new kitchen and the dealer orders them. Thus it takes from six to twelve weeks, often longer, for them to arrive. Custom cabinets are considerably more expensive because of significant differences in construction and finish, and because they are made to order. Because they are made to order, practically anything the customer or designer can imagine can be included in the new kitchen.

Cabinets set the kitchen style

There are four basic kitchen styles: Colonial, Traditional, Provincial and Contemporary.

There also are special styles such as Mediterranean, Oriental, Nautical, Pennsylvania Dutch, Swiss Chalet or others that the imaginative merchandiser might want to feature.

Whatever the style, basic or special, the motif is set by the cabinets. That means the style of the whole kitchen really is set by only two elements, the cabinet doors and the drawer fronts, since these are the most visible elements in the kitchen.

Appliances are visible, but they have no particular influence on style. They simply "go with" the cabinets. Their colors might be varied to blend or highlight certain styles, but their role in kitchen styling always is either supplementary or complementary.

There is wide latitude in the definitions of styling. If a manufacturer wants to call his new line Colonial, Colonial it is, no matter how provincial or contemporary it looks.

With that in mind, let us review the various styles.

Traditional—This is the leader. More manufacturers offer it, and it accounts for 33 percent of all U.S. cabinet production. But many manufacturers include colonial in this category because they are relating to American tradition.

Characteristically, traditional is a somewhat dignified and conservative style featuring a recessed or a raised panel, or at least a false raised panel. Oak carries this style well.

Colonial—This might be called Early American or Country Western, or other similar names. A pegged, board-and-batten door possibly is the ultimate in this styling. V-grooves are common, but pegs alone are usually enough to establish the style even on an otherwise plain door. On the west coast and in the southwest, knotty pine is enough to establish the style, or knotty cedar where a redder look is desired. Colors will be mellow.

Clutter is kept off counter when drawers are outfitted with ventilated metal liners, as for bread and staples.

Storage problem of large flat items is solved with this lid and tray rack. Rack slides out so items can be placed or removed easily.

Lazy susan corner has revolving shelves, individually adjustable. This is for wall cabinet.

Pantry unit has adjustable, self-turning lazy susan rotating shelves.

DESIGN-A-WALL COMPONENTS

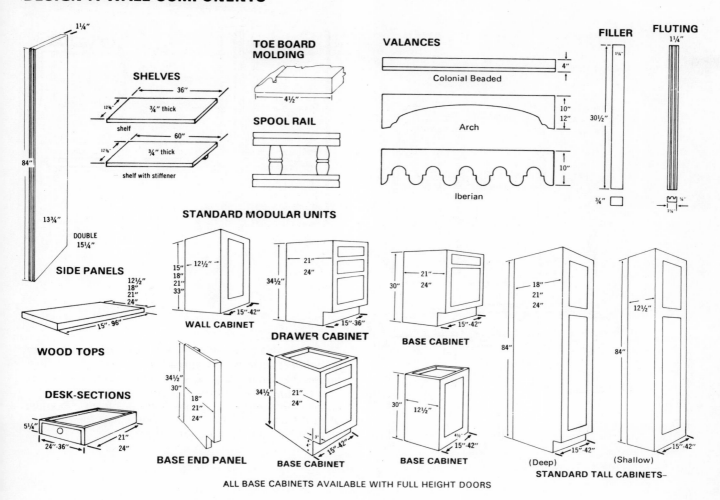

SHELVES

TOE BOARD MOLDING

SPOOL RAIL

VALANCES

Colonial Beaded

Arch

Iberian

FILLER

FLUTING

SIDE PANELS

WOOD TOPS

DESK-SECTIONS

STANDARD MODULAR UNITS

WALL CABINET

DRAWER CABINET

BASE CABINET

BASE END PANEL

BASE CABINET

BASE CABINET

(Deep)   (Shallow)

STANDARD TALL CABINETS—

ALL BASE CABINETS AVAILABLE WITH FULL HEIGHT DOORS

Provincial—This might be French or Italian, with the Italian being somewhat more ornate. Provincial is characterized by moldings on the face of door and drawer front, with arcs at the corners. In cost-cutting versions, the moldings are replaced by a routed groove. Routed grooves also are commonly used on plastic surfaced doors.

Birch and maple are commonly used in provincial styling.

Contemporary—This style, often called modern, is characterized by clean lines and flush or overlay doors.

In all other styles, lip doors are more common. Contemporary doors often are overlay, with a reverse lip to eliminate the need for pulls and knobs. It is in this styling that we often find the solid color cabinetry. It also is a common style used by manufacturers of plastic laminated cabinets.

Mediterranean—This is so popular that perhaps it is inaccurate to call it a special style. It is also difficult

to define, because the Mediterranean region includes Greek, Italian, Moorish, French and many other possible styling influences.

Generally speaking, Mediterranean style is dark and heavy (although it might be light), and quite ornate (although it might be simple). Some builders simply use a dark-toned avocado wood-grain plastic laminated cabinet and call it Mediterranean.

Wood, steel or plastic—and which plastic?

Wood cabinets lead in popularity with home buyers. Plastic laminated cabinets are making slow, steady gains. Steel, a strong leader in the mid-1950s, is no longer a major factor in the residential market although it continues to show some strength in apartments. In fact, at least one widely-respected custom manufacturer still specializes in steel (with wood and plastic options for the doors and drawer fronts).

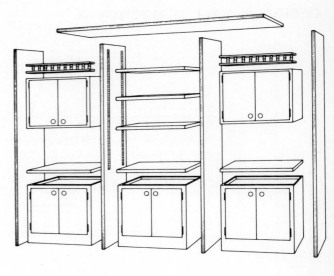

The term "kitchen cabinets" has become a misnomer as builders increasingly spread them throughout the house. Most manufacturers assist with components to adapt them. These pages showing adapting components and how to use them are from a booklet of Rutt Custom Kitchens. The photos that follow show what can de done with them.

New plastics are making an impact. These include foamed polyurethane, polystyrene, nylon, and other types manufactured for surfacing.

SOFTWOODS are more popular in the west and southwest. They include:

Pine—most common, creamy white and very workable. Both Ponderosa and Sugar varieties are used.

Fir—Douglas variety is most widely used, but western cabinet manufacturers also use White.

Knotty pine—again, either Ponderosa, Sugar, or Idaho, but characterized by numerous knots for distinctive styling.

Knotty cedar—quite similar to pine, but reddish in color.

Hemlock—a variety of spruce.

HARDWOODS are more numerous in variety and much more common in cabinetry in the east and midwest where most nationally-distributed cabinets are made. They include:

Birch—the leader by far, heavy, strong and hard with great texture variety, and very inexpensive. White, red, and European are used.

Oak—second in popularity only to birch, it is more expensive but has great appeal to homeowners. It is used in all styles but is especially good for traditional. While the wood itself has a wide color range, it usually is finished dark.

Maple—an excellent, straight-grained material but often with good markings and widely used in colonial styles.

Walnut—strong, with varied patterns, almost always finished medium to dark, but quite expensive.

Birch, beech, alder, ash, cherry, pecan, hickory and red or white lauan (often called Philippine mahogany) are used to varying extents by an appreciable range of manufacturers.

Before moving on to other materials, it should be noted that some of the prettiest teaks and sandalwoods you'll see are not that, but birch or particleboard.

Some major manufacturers take an inexpensive birch and print an exotic finish on it. This is done with big 4-color presses that print full rich coloring on drab birch and impress the grain markings. This technique is also widely used for stereo and television cabinets. It requires very expensive tooling, but the end result is the appearance of exotic woods at bargain-basement prices. The price, naturally, must be a function of volume.

PLASTIC LAMINATES are particularly favored by apartment developers, especially those who keep the property as an investment, because of their great durability, cleanability and visual attractiveness.

They nearly always are wood-grained and the variety is almost infinite. A builder can choose, for example, not just a walnut but from a dozen different walnuts in almost any of the major brands. Or he can choose any exotic woodgrain and it will be almost as true as the natural wood. It should, because it will be precisely printed from an actual color photograph.

The "high pressure" plastic laminates, more or less familiar to builders for the last 25 years, actually are made up of several sheets of heavy Kraft paper, the top sheet printed with the woodgrain or other pattern, and then covered with a transparent melamine plastic which gives the material its great hardness. Traditionally this has been 1/16" thick, and in this thickness it is by far the most common material for kitchen countertops.

Responding to a charge of "over-engineering" (which means "too expensive"), the laminate manufacturers have offered a 1/32" material specifically for vertical surfacing. This is less expensive and highly suitable for kitchen cabinets as well as for walls and table or desk tops that do not receive the wear of a kitchen countertop.

National high-pressure laminate brands are Formica, Pionite, Melamite, Wilson-Art, Parkwood, Micarta, Textolite, DuraBeauty (Consoweld), Enjay Nevamar, and Reliance Panelyte.

Particleboard used for corestock is a finely engineered product relating little to the familiar floor underlayment. This demonstration by Georgia-Pacific shows its versatility and machinability.

Wood lovers charge that these laminates can never really look like wood because of their uniformity of pattern. This is right, perhaps, when one looks at a full 5×12 sheet of plastic laminate, but in a finished cabinet door very few people can tell the difference.

For the plastic laminate manufacturers, competition is not really coming from wood cabinet manufacturers. It is coming from the manufacturers of "poor boy" laminates. This new trend is led by the rigid vinyls, which come in sheet or roll form. This material is much less expensive and provides a reasonably competent substitute for laminates. Its woodgrains are printed by the same type of sophisticated color presses used for the more expensive laminates. Other materials, somewhat similar, include polyesters, used by some cabinet manufacturers, and ABS (acrilonitrile butadiene styrene).

All of these plastic laminates must be adhered to a substrate, or corestock. The substrate might be plywood, styrofoam, or even a honeycomb paper, but more often it will be particleboard. Particleboard as a corestock is not the rough material familiar to builders as floor underlayment. It is a superbly engineered combination of wood particles and resins, almost infinitely variable (to spec) for surface smoothness, weight, screw-holding quality and any other characteristics the cabinet manufacturer might order.

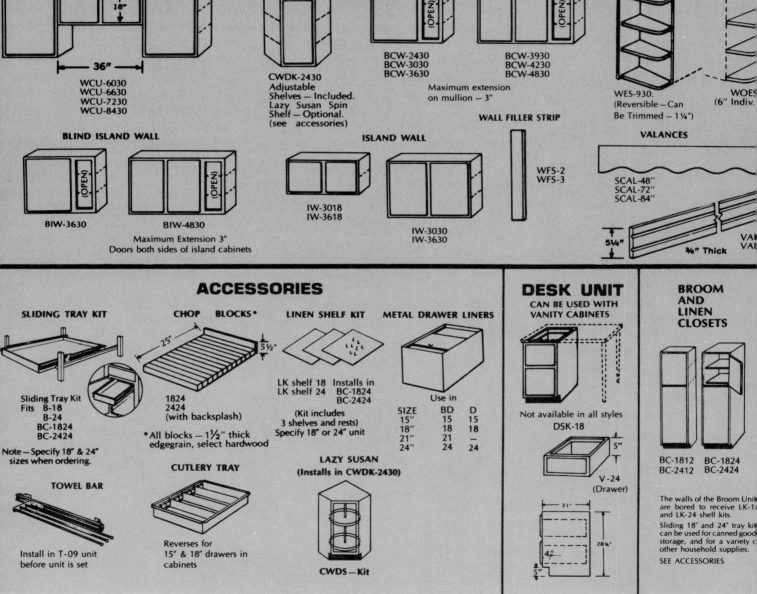

WALL UNITS
First Two Digits Indicate Width in Inches. Second Two Digits Indicate Height in Inches. All Wall Units Are Reversible.

W-3012
W-3312
W-3612

W-3015
W-3315
W-3615

W-2418   W-3618
W-3018   W-4218
W-3318   W-4818

W-2424

23¾"

W-3024   W-4224
W-3624   W-4824

SINGLE DOOR UNIT
Adjustable shelves in some
styles — See spec. sheet.

W-0930   W-1830
W-1230   W-2130
W-1530   W-2430

W-2730   W-39
W-3030   W-42
W-3330   W-48
W-3630

— No Shelves —   — Fixed Shelves —   ← Fixed Shelves

WALL COMBINATION UNITS

18"

36"

WCU-6030
WCU-6630
WCU-7230
WCU-8430

CORNER WALL DIAGONAL

CWDK-2430
Adjustable
Shelves — Included.
Lazy Susan Spin
Shelf — Optional.
(see accessories)

BLIND CORNER WALL

(OPEN)

BCW-2430
BCW-3030
BCW-3630

(OPEN)

BCW-3930
BCW-4230
BCW-4830

Maximum extension
on mullion — 3"

9"

WALL END SHELVES

WES-930.
(Reversible—Can
Be Trimmed — 1¼")

WOES
(6" Indiv.

BLIND ISLAND WALL

(OPEN)

BIW-3630

(OPEN)

BIW-4830

Maximum Extension 3"
Doors both sides of island cabinets

ISLAND WALL

IW-3018
IW-3618

IW-3030
IW-3630

WALL FILLER STRIP

WFS-2
WFS-3

VALANCES

SCAL-48"
SCAL-72"
SCAL-84"

5¼"

¾" Thick   VA
VA

ACCESSORIES

SLIDING TRAY KIT

Sliding Tray Kit
Fits B-18
      B-24
      BC-1824
      BC-2424

Note—Specify 18" & 24"
sizes when ordering.

CHOP BLOCKS*

25"

5½"

1824
2424
(with backsplash)

*All blocks — 1½" thick
edgegrain, select hardwood

LINEN SHELF KIT

LK shelf 18 Installs in
LK shelf 24 BC-1824
            BC-2424

(Kit includes
3 shelves and rests)
Specify 18" or 24" unit

METAL DRAWER LINERS

Use in

SIZE	BD	D
15"	15	15
18"	18	18
21"	21	—
24"	24	24

TOWEL BAR

Install in T-09 unit
before unit is set

CUTLERY TRAY

Reverses for
15" & 18" drawers in
cabinets

LAZY SUSAN
(Installs in CWDK-2430)

CWDS — Kit

DESK UNIT
CAN BE USED WITH
VANITY CABINETS

Not available in all styles
DSK-18

5"

V -24
(Drawer)

21"

28¼"

4"

5"

BROOM
AND
LINEN
CLOSETS

BC-1812   BC-1824
BC-2412   BC-2424

The walls of the Broom Unit
are bored to receive LK-18
and LK-24 shelf kits.

Sliding 18" and 24" tray kits
can be used for canned goods
storage, and for a variety of
other household supplies.

SEE ACCESSORIES

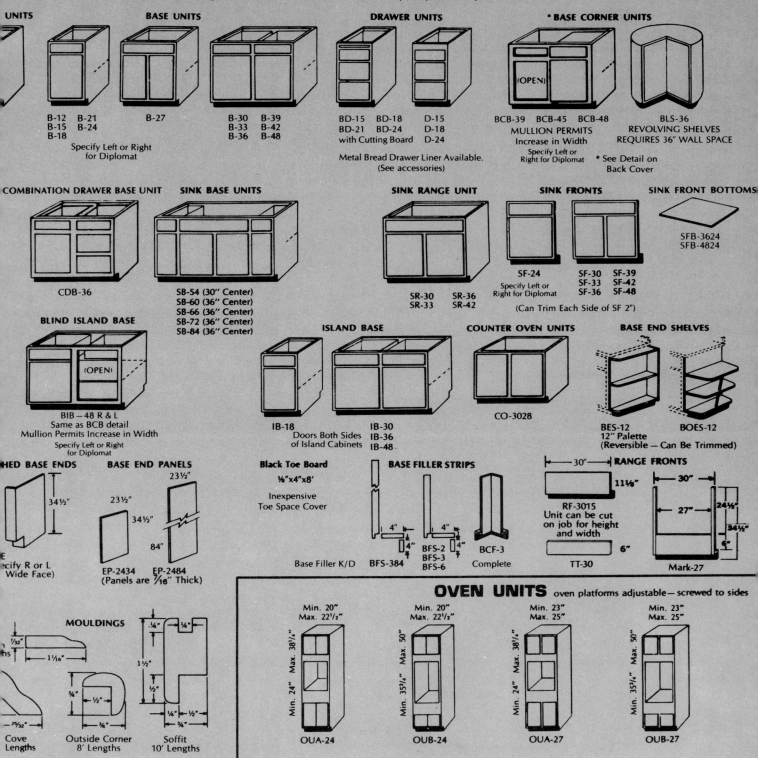

BASE UNITS

First Two Digits Indicate Width in Inches—Base Cabinet is 34½" High and 24" Deep from Face of Frame.
Single Door Base Units Reversible. Except Diplomat Style.

UNITS

BASE UNITS

B-12 B-21
B-15 B-24   B-27
B-18

Specify Left or Right
for Diplomat

DRAWER UNITS

B-30 B-39
B-33 B-42
B-36 B-48

BD-15 BD-18   D-15
BD-21 BD-24   D-18
with Cutting Board   D-24

Metal Bread Drawer Liner Available.
(See accessories)

* BASE CORNER UNITS

(OPEN)

BCB-39 BCB-45 BCB-48
MULLION PERMITS
Increase in Width
Specify Left or
Right for Diplomat

BLS-36
REVOLVING SHELVES
REQUIRES 36" WALL SPACE
* See Detail on
Back Cover

COMBINATION DRAWER BASE UNIT

CDB-36

SINK BASE UNITS

SB-54 (30" Center)
SB-60 (36" Center)
SB-66 (36" Center)
SB-72 (36" Center)
SB-84 (36" Center)

SINK RANGE UNIT

SR-30 SR-36
SR-33 SR-42

SINK FRONTS

SF-24
Specify Left or
Right for Diplomat

SF-30 SF-39
SF-33 SF-42
SF-36 SF-48

(Can Trim Each Side of SF 2")

SINK FRONT BOTTOMS

SFB-3624
SFB-4824

BLIND ISLAND BASE

(OPEN)

BIB—48 R & L
Same as BCB detail
Mullion Permits Increase in Width
Specify Left or Right for
Diplomat

ISLAND BASE

IB-18   IB-30
Doors Both Sides   IB-36
of Island Cabinets IB-48

COUNTER OVEN UNITS

CO-3028

BASE END SHELVES

BES-12   BOES-12
12" Palette
(Reversible — Can Be Trimmed)

HED BASE ENDS

34½"

ecify R or L
Wide Face)

BASE END PANELS

23½"

23½"
34½"
84"

EP-2434 EP-2484
(Panels are 7/16" Thick)

Black Toe Board
⅛"x4"x8'

Inexpensive
Toe Space Cover

BASE FILLER STRIPS

4"   4"
4"   4"
Base Filler K/D   BFS-2   BCF-3
BFS-384   BFS-3   Complete
          BFS-6

RANGE FRONTS

30"
11⅛"
RF-3015
Unit can be cut
on job for height
and width

6"
TT-30

30"
27"   24½"
34½"
6"
Mark-27

OVEN UNITS   oven platforms adjustable—screwed to sides

Min. 20"   Min. 20"   Min. 23"   Min. 23"
Max. 22½"   Max. 22½"   Max. 25"   Max. 25"

Min. 24" Max. 38¼"   Min. 35¾" Max. 50"   Min. 24" Max. 38¼"   Min. 35¾" Max. 50"

OUA-24   OUB-24   OUA-27   OUB-27

MOULDINGS

¼"   ¼"
7/32"
1 1/16"   1½"

¾" ½"   ½"   ½"
²⁵/₃₂"   ¼" ½"
¾"   ¾"

Cove   Outside Corner   Soffit
Lengths   8' Lengths   10' Lengths

Typical specifications sheet of a cabinet manufacturer (in this case, Connor) shows cabinets available with nomenclature and sizes available. Line drawing of each item helps eliminate confusion.

43

Cabinet style sets the kitchen style—Traditional, Colonial, Provincial, Contemporary, Mediterranean or special. And cabinet style is set by the door, but door style is named by the manufacturer and so variations are obvious and confusing. Sometimes a change in hardware makes it a different style. This door is Classic by White-Meyer Wood Products.

c

Colonial styling is exemplified here by, upper right, Provincial Type C by George C. Vaughan and Sons,

and below, Colonial by Scheirich, left, and Williamsburg by Wilson, right.

a

b

a

b

Provincial is characterized by the curves at the corners of the design. Shown here are Royal Coach

by Grabill, left above, and Mission Oak by Raygold, right above.

a

b

Contemporary styles are clean, uncluttered, often have no knobs or pulls on doors and drawers, as with the drawers of the first example here. Left,

Luxuria by Long-Bell; right, Contemporary Walnut by Wilson.

Mediterranean styles derive from all of the many cultural influences that border that sea, and so generally are more decorative than other styles, as *these examples indicate. Shown here are, left to right above, Espana by Yatron Bros., Granada by Keystone, and Venetian Oak by Springfield Cabinet.*

All of these plastic laminates are good materials for cabinets, as are all of the corestocks mentioned, but there are some traps the builder must avoid.

Any plastic laminated cabinet door needs a backing sheet. Otherwise, the construction is out of balance and warping can follow. The flocking or cheap paint sometimes applied to the back will not do the job.

Also, in any market area there always is a peripheral assortment of suppliers who prey on the builders who want the cheapest price. These are the ones who will offer unbalanced doors. Their vinyl surfacing often does not have proper adhesives. The result of this is that the vinyl, which has been molded to the door with heat, attempts to revert back to its original form. This is called "creep," a term a housewife might also use to describe the builder when she sees the vinyl shrinking from the corners of her cabinets and leaving the wood exposed.

This is a common problem, because vinyl itself is so inexpensive that it attracts the kind of cabinet maker who cuts corners. The solution is to stick with reputable manufacturers.

In recent years, the texture of high pressure plastic laminates has been expanded to true 3-dimensional surfaces. Nevamar pioneered this development with a "Cameo" pattern, and now several manufacturers offer 3-dimensional slate patterns in either white or black.

The 3-dimensional feature always has been available

with the other laminates. A great advantage of vinyl, for example, is that it can be vacuum-formed to conform to any mold. In this process the sheet of vinyl is heated to a point of pliability, then sucked down by vacuum not only to cover the mold but to surround it. This yields a shell that is fully edged with corners turned, all one piece with no joining problem. This shell then needs only to be slipped over the corestock, adhered, and backed for balance.

The mold might be a specially carved or built-up wood master. It might be the cabinet door of a competitor that is being copied. Whatever it is, if the vacuum-forming is done properly the resultant vinyl shell will be a precise copy, mirroring all 3-dimensional aspects. Since the woodgrain or other pattern will already have been printed on the underside (so it will be protected against scratches by the vinyl on top) the door will need no further finishing except for the back.

This practice of printing the woodgrain or other pattern on the underside is called "reverse printing." Its only disadvantage is that the adhesive that bonds the vinyl shell to the corestock does not grip the vinyl itself, but the ink on the underside of the vinyl. Modern adhesives and bonding techniques make this a minor problem. But it does mean the job must be done right.

Some vinyls are surface-printed, so the bond is direct from corestock to vinyl. This helps the bond, but makes

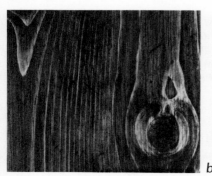

a

b

c

d

e

f

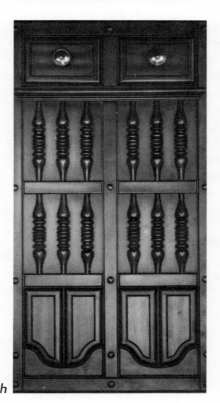

g

h

i

the surface more susceptible to scratching. Some suppliers now are solving both of these problems by surface-printing the vinyl and overlaying it with another sheet of clear vinyl. It solves the problems, but raises the cost.

STEEL, as has been mentioned, is no longer a major factor in residential kitchen cabinets. As of this writing, there are only two quality custom steel manufacturers in the field, and there are several others who specialize in the apartment market. The apartment market, of course, is a price market.

Low-priced steel cabinets find it very hard to compete on a price basis with low-priced wood cabinets.

At the expensive end of the steel market, cabinet manufacturers offer a strong steel framework with options of steel, wood, plastic laminated or all-plastic doors and drawer fronts.

At the other end of the market there is a steel framework with steel doors, but sometimes the steel doors have vinyl plastic inlays to give them a semblance of wood. These inlays not only make the cabinets more acceptable to homeowners, they also permit modernization of the doors in later years through exchange of the inserts for new ones.

Steel is structurally rigid, strong, durable, and warp-free. Everything good that the steel people say about steel as a cabinet material is true.

There is nothing wrong with steel, except that most customers want wood.

THE NEW MOLDED PLASTICS have just commenced their invasion of the cabinet market. They include polyurethane, polystyrene, and nylon, and there undoubtedly will be others. These materials are formulated in the Research & Development labs of the petrochemical companies who develop combinations of resins and binders, and then start scrambling for applications. In the scramble, the cabinet market always shows up because it offers a potential annual market of some 100,000,000 cabinet doors, plus drawer fronts.

Generally, polyurethane is best for relatively short production runs, polystyrene for long runs, nylon for very long runs. This evaluation is related directly to tooling costs. Tooling for polyurethane is quite cheap. For the other materials it is very expensive. Quality of the end product, for all three, is excellent.

True value of these plastics is in the stylistic effects that can be achieved at a reasonable price.

If considered as a price product, they cost about

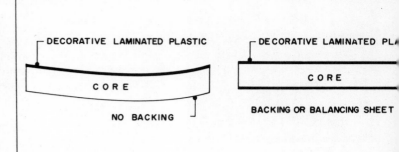

Plastic laminate, when used for cabinet doors or any other unsupported application, must have a backing sheet to balance the substrate for dimensional stability. Otherwise it will warp. Countertops do not need backing sheets because they are held stable by the base cabinets.

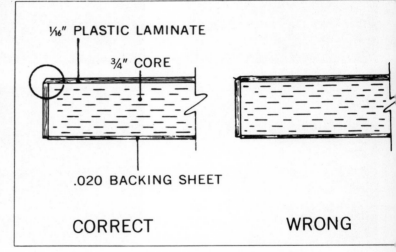

When self-edging is used, it should be applied first, before top surface, so top surface covers the edge-band.

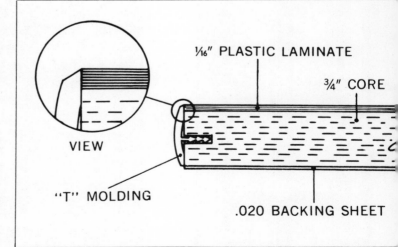

If T-edging is used it is applied after top surface. It must be precisely indexed with top of laminate.

50% more than birch. Styles that would be impossible with any wood because of dimensional instability, such as in an interwoven cane door, can be achieved easily with any of these molded plastics with realism that defies detection. When the difference is only about $1 per door, the high style of the cane often is desirable.

These plastics are finished like wood, using the same equipment and materials. They are getting to be very common on bathroom vanities, because only four or five molds can supply an entire vanity line. Their success has been more limited in kitchen cabinets because the mold needs multiply. It is not unusual for a cabinet manufacturer to have as many as 400 or 500 variations in size and style, and this would mean that many different molds for a plastic line.

Marriages of wood and plastics are becoming common—plain wood doors are decorated with plastic moldings to create Provincial, Mediterranean, or other styles. This is a low-priced way to get a highly-styled cabinet.

CABINET CONSTRUCTION varies among manufacturers to some extent, but it is fairly well standardized for stock cabinets.

The main components are *front frames, doors, drawers and drawer fronts, end panels, backs, bottoms, shelves* and *hardware.*

Horizontal members of the *front frame* are called *rails.* Vertical members of the front frame are *stiles.* Interior horizontal framing members are *subrails,* and interior vertical framing members are *substiles.* A kick rail at the bottom of the base cabinet, recessed 3" behind the front frame, is called the *toe kick.*

Front frames are usually made of 1/2" to 3/4" hardwood, and the rails and stiles usually are doweled or mortise-and-tenoned, with both glue and staples added for rigidity.

End panels are usually constructed of hardwood plywood, 3/16" or 1/4", glued to 3/4" side frames. Sometimes a 1/2" or thicker end panel is used without a side frame, and usually tongue-and-grooved into the front frame.

Doors typically are 3/4" or 7/8" but this is subject to wide variation. They might be hollow or have cores of particleboard, wood, high density fiber, plastic, paper honeycomb, or other material. As mentioned before, doors set the style, and drawer fronts match the doors, so this is the area where manufacturers are creative.

Backs usually are 1/8" hardboard or 3-ply plywood, and the backs have *mounting rails* or *hanging strips* at top and bottom for screwing cabinets into the wall.

Tops and *bottoms* generally are made of 3-ply or 5-ply hardwood plywood, 1/4" to 1/2" thick, dadoed into the sides and interlocked into the hanging strips of wall cabinets.

Shelves are 1/2" to 3/4" thick and might be lumber, plywood or particleboard. Increasingly they are vinyl-laminated for easy cleaning. They usually are adjustable.

Conventional *drawers* have hardwood lumber sides and backs with plywood bottoms. Sides usually are connected to the front and back with a lock or rabbeted joint, although more expensive cabinets go to multiple dovetailing. Drawer bottoms are dadoed into the sides, front, and back.

Some cabinet companies now are using molded polystyrene drawers, all one piece except for the front, with rounded corners for easy cleaning.

A few companies offer cabinets unfinished, but most are finished, some in very sophisticated equipment systems. Fundamentally, all surfaces are well sanded before a penetrating stain is applied. After the stain is dry, one or more coats of sealer are applied and then all nail holes are filled with a suitable putty. A thorough sanding follows, and then one or more finish coats. In finishing, some factories use spray gun systems, some use curtain coaters which lay on the finish in controlled mil thickness, while others use immersion systems. Finishing lines usually are conveyorized with the lines carrying finished parts directly through heat tunnels for drying.

TYPES OF CABINETS can be grouped into three categories: *Base, wall* and *miscellaneous.* The standard base cabinet is 34-1/2" high, so the addition of the countertop will bring it to an even 36". Depths vary from 23" to 24-1/2", depending on the manufacturer. Base cabinets are offered in 3" modules from 12" to 24" for a single door cabinet, and 27" to 48" for a double door cabinet. Special cabinets for the sink or a built-in cooktop range from 24" to 48" wide. Also relatively standard is a sink base combination with four doors and a drawer over the door on either end, with the center section blank, of course, for sink or cooktop, and these vary from 54" to 96" in width.

The standard *wall cabinet* is 30" high and 12" or 13" deep, depending on the manufacturer. Wall filler cabinets, designed to fit above the refrigerator or window or for other special purposes, might be 11",

Cabinet Accessories

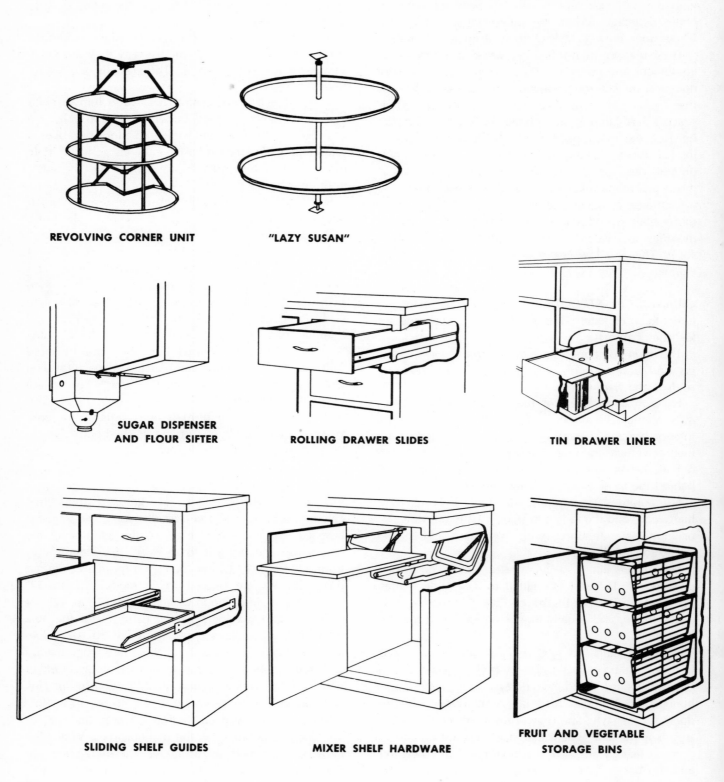

REVOLVING CORNER UNIT

"LAZY SUSAN"

SUGAR DISPENSER AND FLOUR SIFTER

ROLLING DRAWER SLIDES

TIN DRAWER LINER

SLIDING SHELF GUIDES

MIXER SHELF HARDWARE

FRUIT AND VEGETABLE STORAGE BINS

12", 15", 18" or 24" high. There also are wall combination cabinets with 30" doors on the ends and 18" doors in between. All of these match the widths of the base cabinets.

Two other fairly common cabinets are revolving-shelf (or lazy susan) cabinets, base or wall, and blank corner cabinets. The revolving shelf cabinets require 21", 24" or 27" along each wall for the wall cabinet, or 33", 36", or 42" along each wall for a base cabinet.

Blank corner cabinets are for turning a corner where another run of cabinets will join at a right angle. They are blank (no door or drawer) in the area where the other cabinets must butt up against them. Base blank corner cabinets might be 24", 36", 39", 42", 48", 60", 66", 72" or 84". There is one door and drawer in sizes over 24", multiple doors and drawers at 60" and over. Wall blank corner cabinets run in 6" modules from 24" to 48" and from 60" to 84".

Miscellaneous cabinets include:

A *refrigerator cabinet,* 36", 39" or 42" wide with the opening varying according to the size of the refrigerator;

An *oven cabinet* for built-in ovens, in widths of 24", 27", 30", or 33", with cutout sizes that must vary according to the countless specifications of oven manufacturers;

Utility or broom cabinets in widths of 24", 30" and 36", and depths of 12", 13" and 18" as well as standard base depths.

All of these come in the standard 84" height, but oven cabinets also come in 66" height without doors at the top. The broom cabinets also are often outfitted with hardware for lazy susan shelves or special fold-out pantry cabinets.

Base cabinets may be obtained without drawers, with one drawer, or with all drawers and no door. Sink or range fronts also are available, without full cabinets. Both wall and base cabinets are available with doors on both sides for entry from either side, for use in peninsulas such as between the kitchen and the dining or living area.

INTERIOR FITTINGS are to cabinets what accessories are to cars—all the little options that add function, organization, utility, and convenience and that make the difference between ordinary and great. Unfortunately, builders pass them up because they add to cost and homeowners never know about them.

These fittings are much more widely used in Europe.

Builders, architects and homeowners often return from abroad raving about these little kitchen conveniences and wondering why U.S. kitchens don't copy them, actually they always have been available here from both stock and custom cabinet manufacturers, and there are indeed many, many options.

There are towel racks, sugar bins, flour bins, vegetable bins, vertical tray storage cabinets, bread drawer liners, pan racks, slide-in table tops that disappear into the cabinetry, lazy susan assemblies for both base and wall units, electric mixer shelves counterbalanced with springs to pop up into place, slide-out maple cutting boards, to name just a few. There are even wheeled serving carts that roll into the cabinet run where they look like just another cabinet, silver drawer organizers, cup and plate storage organizers, in-cabinet or under-cabinet spice racks, and bar organizers, etc.

All of these are fitted into the cabinets or into the drawers by the cabinet manufacturer. In some cases he provides a special cabinet or special shelving for them, in other cases it is a matter of finding appropriate hardware and correctly installing it. In all cases these fixtures add special appeal to the kitchen and make it much more convenient for the housewife who will use it.

HARDWARE, generally, is a tremendously varied part of the kitchen cabinetry that performs many functions, both utilitarian and decorative.

Some of the possibilities of utility hardware are indicated in the previous section on options. There are many more. For example, drawers of low cost cabinets often operate with wood sliding on wood. They will work all right when new, but will be far less than satisfactory when humidity is high or as they get older.

In contrast, both simple and elaborate slides are available. These might have nylon sliding on nylon, low-priced but with excellent results, or finely engineered ball-bearing wheels in metal channels. It is a small part of the total kitchen, but a big factor in customer satisfaction as the years go by.

The pulls and knobs, and sometimes the hinges on cabinet doors, are decorative as well as functional. In fact, one hardware manufacturer calls its line ''Cabinet Jewelry.'' And it is.

Knobs and pulls, for the drawers and doors, usually are metal and might be finished as brass, bronze, brushed chrome, antique pewter, or enamel. Some

Good Installation Essential

1

Cabinets must be attached to studs for full support. Studs are usually located 16″ on center. Locate studs with stud finder, tapping with hammer or nail driven through plaster at height that will be hidden by cabinets. Cabinets must always be attached to walls with screws. **Never use nails!**

2

Cabinets must be installed perfectly level — from a standpoint of function as well as appearance. Find the highest point of floor with the use of a level.

3

Using a level or straightedge, find the high spots on the wall on which cabinets are to be hung. Some high spots can be removed by sanding. Otherwise, it will be necessary to "shim" to provide a level and plumb installation.

4

Using the highest point on the floor, measure up the wall to a height of 84″. This height, 84″, is the top height of wall cabinets, oven and broom cabinets. 84″ cabinets can be cut down to 81″.

The most expensive cabinets made will be failures if not properly installed. And the cheapest cabinets can give good service if they are installed right. Cabinet manufacturers realize this, and all give

5

On the walls where cabinets are to be installed, remove baseboard and chair rail. This is required for a flush fit.

6

Start your installation in one corner. First assemble the base corner unit, then adding one unit on each side of the corner unit. This — as a unit — can be installed in position. Additional cabinets are then added to each side as required.

7

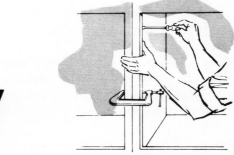

"C" clamps should be used in connecting cabinets together to obtain proper alignment. Drill 2 or 3 holes through ½″ end panels. Holes should be drilled through to adjoining cabinet. Secure T-nut and secure with 1½″ bolt. Draw up snugly. If you prefer you may drill through side of front frame as well as "lead hole" into abutting cabinet, insert screws and draw up snugly.

detailed instructions for installation. The accompanying sequence is from the installation manual of Kitchen Kompact, the giant of the industry. (Also overleaf)

8

Each cabinet — as it is installed to the wall — should be checked front to back and also across the front edge with a level. Be certain that the front frame is plumb. If necessary, use shims to level the cabinets. Base cabinets should be attached with screws into wall studs. For additional support and to prevent back rail from "bowing," insert block between cabinet back and wall. After bases are installed cover toe kick area with material that is provided.

9

Attach counter top on base cabinets. After installation, cover counter tops with cartons to prevent damage while completing installation.

10

Wall cabinets should then be installed, beginning with a corner unit as described in step #6. Screw through hanging strips built into backs of cabinets at both top and bottom. Place them ¾" below top and ¾" above bottom shelf from inside of cabinet. Adjust only loosely at first so that final adjustments can be made.

11

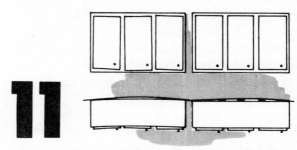

Wall cabinets should be checked with level on cabinet front, sides, and bottom to insure that cabinets are plumb and level. It might be necessary to shim at wall and between cabinets to correct for uneven walls or floors. After cabinets and doors are perfectly aligned, tighten all screws.

Problem Doors:

There are very few "perfect" conditions where floors and walls are exactly level and plumb. Therefore, it is necessary to correct this by proper "shimming" so that the cabinet is not racked or twisted and so that cabinet doors are properly aligned.

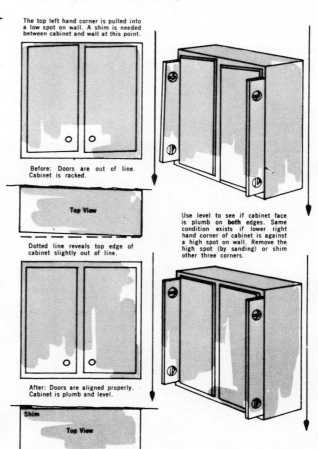

The top left hand corner is pulled into a low spot on wall. A shim is needed between cabinet and wall at this point.

Before: Doors are out of line. Cabinet is racked.

Top View

Dotted line reveals top edge of cabinet slightly out of line.

Use level to see if cabinet face is plumb on **both** edges. Same condition exists if lower right hand corner of cabinet is against a high spot on wall. Remove the high spot (by sanding) or shim other three corners.

After: Doors are aligned properly. Cabinet is plumb and level.

Shim

Top View

knobs and pulls are ceramic while others are plastic. The latter usually are finished to resemble ceramics. They might be solid colors or they might have delicate inlays. One hardware manufacturer has a "Mod" line with colored knobs with square or circular backplates with mondrian designs, geometrics, or swirls. These can work chromatic magic in brightening up a run of cabinets that otherwise might be dull.

Cabinets usually come with standard hardware selected by the manufacturer. However, the builder, architect or customer can ask to see options, and usually some options are available at no extra cost. In some cases the hardware is an integral part of the cabinet design, and the cabinet manufacturer will be reluctant to change it. In these cases, the manufacturer usually is right. He has spent a lot of money developing a design and he doesn't want to see it changed.

CABINET INSTALLATION is the true key to success in any kitchen.

If installed properly, the cheapest cabinets available give better service than poorly installed expensive cabinets. Proper installation is the one nonvarying essential, and as a precept it also is the most abused.

Cabinets must be installed level, plumb and true.

This means the walls and floor must be checked for high spots and low spots, and corners must be checked for square. High spots sometimes can be sanded down. Low spots must be shimmed.

If, on installation, one corner of a cabinet is pulled into a low spot in the wall, the cabinet will be racked and the door will hang crooked. If it is a cabinet with multiple doors, all of the doors will be crooked.

Cabinets should be installed always from a corner, never toward a corner. C clamps should be used to hold them alligned perfectly as they are screwed to each other. They must be attached to the wall with screws, never with nails, and the screws must go into the studs.

Base cabinets should be installed first, and then the countertop should be installed. Cartons then should be placed on top of the installed base cabinets to protect them while the wall cabinets are installed, and wall cabinets also should start with a corner.

(Note: Some inexperienced installers know that a kitchen always is *designed* starting with the sink, which usually is in the center of a run of cabinets. This is one reason why they sometimes try to install them that way, but this is wrong.)

Again, make sure the installers are expert at their work. Poor installation can ruin the highest-quality cabinets, and a bad kitchen can make it a bad house.

Simple, roomy kitchen is fully carpeted, gains extra distinction with wood treatment at window to match cabinets. This is Centennial line marking 100th anniversary of Connor Forest Industries.

4

Major and Minor Appliances

By definition and by function, the major home appliances are the range, the refrigerator, the freezer, the dishwasher, the washer, and the dryer.

The latter two are not kitchen appliances, although they sometimes are placed in the kitchen. More properly they belong in a utility room or a basement or, ideally, in the main bathroom if space permits.

Other very important appliances that belong in any modern kitchen are a ventilating hood over any cooking appliance, and a garbage disposer.

There are some other appliances that can add greatly to homeowner convenience and lift a kitchen far above the ordinary. These include the microwave oven, built-in warming drawer or other food warmer, built-in mixing center, toaster, can opener, and under-the-counter ice maker. There also is the barbecue grill, which might be integral with the range or cooktop or, better, separated from the main cooking area as an added appliance.

And there are, of course, the trash compactors. These are rapidly getting to be standard appliances, but they still are relatively new.

Some communities have challenged them on an ecological basis, fearing that their community incinerating facilities may not be able to handle their compacted "bricks" of trash, and have even gone so far as to legislate against their use.

On the other hand, the compacted trash makes excellent landfill. So where a builder runs into a local incinerator problem, there are alternatives he can investigate.

There's no question on consumer attitudes. They like compactors. And as a family grows to four or more, this appliance becomes much more significant.

There are other areas to be watched on a month-to-month basis. Some water purification systems are already on the market and others might come out at any time. Also check air purification and humidity control systems. As new appliances are introduced, they must be weighed for value, utility, and customer appeal.

Every category of appliances presents its own range of choices and decisions. In this chapter we will consider the available options, category by category.

Ranges

No other category of kitchen appliances enjoys the variety of cooking appliances, in sizes available, configurations, and features.

Free-standing—a range that stands by itself, independent of the wall or cabinets on either side. It can be a single oven model, with broiler, or a double-oven with eye-level oven or broiler, even with a microwave oven. These come now with squared sides so they fit neatly against adjacent countertops. The common size is 30" wide, but choices range from 19" to 40". They can be gas or electric, with or without backsplash, with controls in the front, on top along the side, or on a backsplash.

Built-in—again either single or double cavity for the oven which must be fitted into a wall cabinet built for this purpose, with or without a microwave component. Companion to the wall oven is the built-in cooktop, and these also are offered in a wide variety of configurations, gas or electric, and many sizes. The built-in system offers the greatest flexibility in kitchen design. However, it entails cutting precisely-sized holes in the oven cabinet and the countertop according

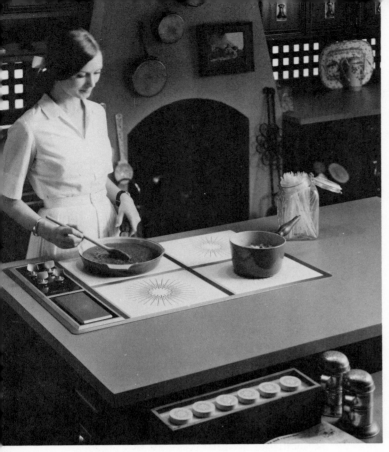

Built-in installations have most design flexibility. This Tappan glass-top was installed in island. Built-in wall oven is out of traffic area. Corning glass-top also is in island, with double wall-oven showing in background.

to specifications for the particular model being installed, so great care must be taken to check the specs against the model numbers. There are about 60 manufacturers of built-in cooking equipment, each with from two to a dozen models, and specs vary widely.

Slide-in—this is basically a free-standing range, but with the side panels left off and engineered to fit snugly against the countertop, or even overlap it, for a built-in look. Nevertheless, it rests on the floor. It is popular with builders and in less-expensive modernization, and sizes range from a minimal 19" to a more standard 30". It can have one or two ovens and can be either basic or deluxe. It might fit under or against a backsplash that is continuous with the countertops, and some are made to be fitted to the cutout backsplash of the countertop on either side.

Drop-in—a variation of the slide-in, the drop-in does not rest on the floor. Flanges rest on the countertop on either side, and it is supported from there. Special cabinets are available to fit under it for a more built-in look, although it might extend all the way down to the kick space.

Stack-on—a type that might not always be on the market at a given time, the stack-on consists of a built-in cooktop and superstructure with an eye-level oven. Although configuration limits the range to a single cavity oven, one manufacturer has had great success by combining a stack-on with a matching built-in dishwasher that fits directly beneath it, an innovative space-saver.

The specials—There are other models which do fit into the foregoing categories, but they are so different that they require special mention.

One is Pan-O-Matic, a "topless" cooktop. Actually it is a powered panel that rises behind the countertop, in the backsplash area, and into which portable cooking vessels are plugged. The vessels include wired pots and pans, engineered for use with this system, and there also are standard convenience outlets on the panel. The panel is luminous and rises to an eye-level shelf which holds all controls, and the upper surface of which serves as a warming shelf. The wired utensils are stored in cabinets beneath.

The other special product is the Jenn-Air, a cooktop with integral down-draft ventilation which obviates the need for a conventional ventilating hood. There are matching eye-level ovens to go with this, and a slide-in model is available with oven below.

Free-standing ranges now have squared corners for a built-in look. They can fit flush against cabinetry or stand by themselves. This, by Modern Maid, has two continuous-clean ovens, "smoothie" glass-ceramic cooking surface, and built-in "Vent-Pak" that vents entire range.

Slide-in ranges might come with or without side panels, and squared corners give a built-in look. With side panels they can be free-standing. This is by Caloric. Some come without backsplash, fit snugly under countertop backsplash for more of a built-in look.

Drop-in ranges must rest on a cabinet at bottom, as these do, or hang from flanges that extend over countertop on either side. The model shown, by Corning, has a backsplash. The model by Jenn-Air must be cut into countertop, has no backsplash of its own. The Jenn-Air has down-draft ventilation through grill in center, needs no hood above. Optional kit available to convert to free-standing, with backsplash.

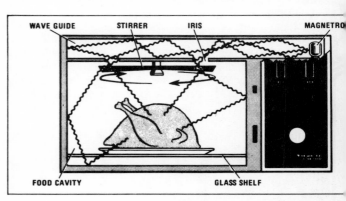

Yes, this is a cooking range, but behind the countertop! Tappan's Pan-O-Matic is a "topless" cooktop occupying practically no counter space. Matched utensils are stored in cabinet below, have built-in rigid male plug that plugs into black base at bottom. Controls at top match the six outlets at base, and top serves as warming shelf.

Sketch showing operation of microwave oven.

Deluxe version of Thermador's "Thermatronic" built-in microwave oven includes the microwave at the top, self-cleaning oven at the bottom, and electrically heated warming drawer in middle.

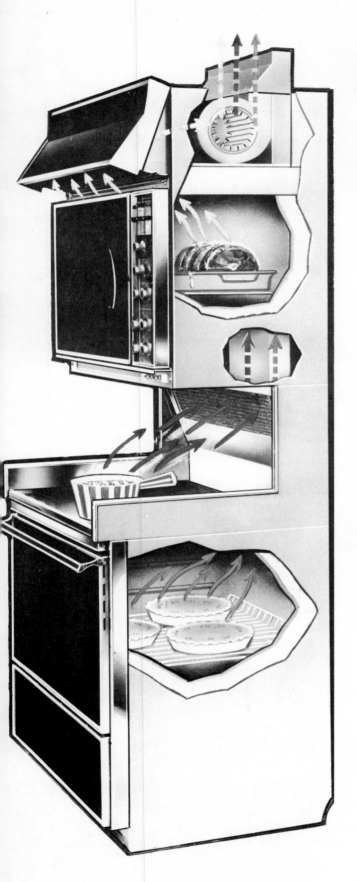

Cleanability of modern cooktops is demonstrated with this Modern Maid model. Top flips up exposing only a shallow pan to be wiped.

Catalytic continuous-cleaning is demonstrated by applying special frit on one side, not on other, then setting oven to baking temperature for a couple of hours.

Drawing shows how blower at top can vent entire Modern Maid range. Hood at top tilts out when in use.

Compu-Timer is name of new computerized control for Modern Maid oven, available on either gas or electric, built-in or free-standing. To operate you set weight in pounds on first dial, press start button on second dial, select and set degree of doneness on third dial (from reference chart for various meats printed on control panel) and then set heat in degrees. This also has cook-and-hold feature, and clock with digital readout.

Another version of drop-in range has non-supporting cabinet below. Range is suspended from flanges that extend over countertop. This is new Tappan model.

Tappan stack-on range is suspended from countertop by flanges, has self-cleaning eye-level oven.

Revolutionary new electric range with unique "touch controls will bring computer technology into the kitchen for everyday use by the homemaker, simplifying home cooking operations as never before. New range employs an illuminated digital information display system more commonly known as a visual "readout." It replaces some of the conventional electro- mechanical components with a glass touch panel, integrated circuits and solid state components. (Frigidaire)

CONVENIENCE FEATURES of cooking appliances are as plentiful and varied as the configurations.

Cooktops, which might come with from two to six burners, often have thermostatic controls on at least one burner.

Cooktops can be purchased with griddle and grill inserts, which might be in the center or along the side.

They feature varying degrees of cleanability. Some detach completely to leave only a smooth-surfaced pan to be cleaned. Many feature top surfaces that can be raised, with a drop bar to hold them upright for cleaning underneath.

Automatic timers are common. It should be noted, though, that many less-expensive models have built-in timers that will signal a lapse of time, but do not control the cooktop or the oven.

Some ovens feature simultaneous over-and-under broiling. Some have their own built-in exhaust systems. Most have optional rotisseries and temperature-sensing probes.

The real aristocrats of ovens will have such complete automatic controls that a housewife can put her meal in the oven, set a time for it to start cooking hours later, set a time for it to stop cooking, and from then on it will hold a keep-warm temperature (about 170 degrees) until she and her family return home in the evening.

The cook-and-hold feature is available even without the more elaborate start-and-stop controls described.

One manufacturer even provides an instant hot water tap on the backplate of the range, so the housewife needn't go to the sink for cooking water.

SELF-CLEANING is probably the greatest oven feature to be developed in recent years. Through the years, cleaning the oven has been the housewife's most-abhorred kitchen chore. Now ovens clean themselves.

There are two types of self-cleaning ovens, pyrolytic and catalytic, and they should be explained.

In the pyrolytic system, the oven is heated to a temperature range between 900 and 1,000 degrees and the mess in the oven is incinerated. This leaves only a fine ash to be wiped off.

The catalytic system employs a coating on inside surfaces which, in effect, lets the oven clean itself in normal cooking ranges through action of the catalytic coating. This system usually is referred to as "continuous clean," or "stay clean."

The pyrolytic system adds about $100 to the selling price of a range. The catalytic system adds only about $25. But there are many other considerations besides cost.

The pyrolytic system, simply stated, requires raising interior temperature to the 900–1000-degree range for a period of from 30 to 90 minutes. The heat-up and cool-down time, however, makes this a period of from two to four hours. The time depends on soil density.

The heat must be raised and the burning must take place under fully-controlled conditions, and this means the oven must be brought to full-heat slowly.

Also, the burning process requires a controlled input of air for proper oxidation. This is done usually through control of the air space under the oven door, or air passages in the lower part of the door. If too much air is admitted the temperature will rise too fast. This is why all pyrolytic oven doors become locked when the temperature is over 625 degrees. Any opening of the door after that point would permit a dangerous inrush of oxygen.

Pyrolytic ovens also have to be made somewhat smaller than others. This is because the usual organic binders in common insulation break down at pyrolytic temperatures. Inorganic high-temperature binders are needed, and this makes the insulation package bulkier.

In the catalytic process, interior oven surfaces are coated with a porcelain frit that contains a catalyst. This gives the surfaces a porosity that enables them to retain oxygen. At higher (baking) temperatures this results in a slow oxidation that disposes of the oven soil.

Much oven cooking, however, is not baking, so obviously the system does not work as totally and automatically as indicated. Nevertheless, the oven can be set for "bake" for a few hours after cooking is completed, and then it will clean itself.

Both systems are available from most range manufacturers, but because of the lack of design problems and because of the price advantage, the catalytic system probably offers a greater variety of choices among models.

DO THEY REALLY CLEAN THEMSELVES? I will state here, categorically, that both pyrolytic and catalytic self cleaners will do the job they claim to do.

But no manufactured product is beyond the range of human culpability. Either a self-cleaner or a continuous-cleaner will do its job precisely as its manufacturer claims. It will *not* correct your own errors. If there are big spills in cooking, these must be wiped up before cleaning begins.

But the cleaning function always needs three factors: Time, oxygen and temperature. In the case of a big spill, no oxygen will be available at the center of the spillage and it could take many cleanings for that spillage to disappear.

Roper is so confident of its continuous-cleaner that it puts the catalytic finish right onto the oven interior, not onto removable panels. They can do this only because they are sure. Modern Maid, a pioneer in gas self-cleaning, has abandoned that concept totally in favor of continuous cleaning. Again, an affirmation of faith in the process.

The answer is, don't permit yourself to be oversold by the salesman. Both processes will work, but you must follow directions.

It should be noted also that the literature with a continuous-clean oven does not claim total cleanliness. It claims that, if directions are followed, the oven will have "the appearance" of being clean.

But cleaning starts to take place at about 350 degrees. For extra cleaning, you might have to turn it up to 450 degrees empty for up to two hours.

THE NEW SMOOTH GLASS COOKTOPS are an exciting development in cooking appliances. They are attractive, totally uncluttered, effective, and reduce surface cleaning to a minimum.

Actually, the idea of a smooth cooktop is not new. It was common in grandmother's day when much cooking still was done with wood and coal. The only breaks in the smooth metal top of the range were for the slots into which a lifter was placed to remove the burner covers.

Corning Glass brought the idea up to date with the development of a glass ceramic, Pyroceram, in 1957. There now are different versions by several other manufacturers.

The material has interesting features. For example, it transmits heat vertically to the cooking vessel, but heat does not migrate horizontally through the glass ceramic material. While the area of the burners can be hot enough for all cooking operations, at the same time the areas immediately surrounding the burners remain cool to the touch.

As a safety factor, heated areas over the burners turn a yellowish color to warn against careless touching. This coloration disappears as the glass cools. While some critics have expressed the fear that a hot surface might be touched accidentally by a child, there really is no more danger of this than there is from a conventional electric range burner.

Other critics have worried about breakability. But Corning is so confident of the strength of its unit that it has gone to a single sheet of glass over the full 30-inch width of the range. Other manufacturers, in deference to the worriers, put a separate sheet of glass over each burner so that, in the unlikely event of breakage, only that one part would have to be replaced.

In actual use, the main difference between the Corning product and all others is that Corning provides a matched set of cooking vessels, also of Pyroceram, with bottoms that are perfectly flat and ground to mate with the smooth surface of the cooktop. The recommendation is that no other cooking vessels be used.

The primary reason for this is control. All materials have temperature limitations, and this includes metals as well as glass ceramics. And while these limitations are subject to change according to the progress in the R&D departments, at this writing the limits are around 600 to 700 Celsius (degrees Centigrade.)

A bright aluminum saucepan with a wavy bottom could easily raise the rangetop temperature above the limit, particularly at times when the housewife forgets and lets it boil dry.

Corning uses temperature control on each of the four elements, with a sensor cycling the heat on and off according to the setting. The precise control requires excellent thermal contact with the cooking vessel, hence the special vessels which insure this contact.

The top will cook with other vessels, including metal, but if the bottoms are not flat for good contact, there could be a control problem.

MICROWAVE COOKING is not the newest marvel in the kitchen but it certainly is one of the most exciting. These microwaves are electromagnetic waves of energy, similar to radio waves, light waves, or radar. Microwave cooking was, in fact, discovered in the 1940's by a radar technician who inadvertently left some uncooked popcorn exposed to radar waves. When the corn started popping a whole new system of cooking was conceived.

There are many microwave ovens on the market in countertop, built-in, and free-standing configurations.

Why is it exciting? Because it is instant cooking. Four strips of bacon that take 23 minutes to cook conventionally take four minutes in a countertop microwave. Roast beef medium takes about eight minutes per pound and frozen shrimp is cooked in six minutes.

It is cooking without pots and pans. Cooking can be done on a paper plate or a glass or plastic dish, and these materials do not heat up except from the heat of the food itself.

The waves pass through paper, glass or plastic with no effect. Since they are reflected by metal, metal cannot be placed in a microwave oven. Foods absorb the microwaves, and the waves cause food molecules to rotate 180 degrees with such rapidity that they cause heat from the friction, and this heat causes cooking.

In conventional cooking food is surrounded by heat and heat must penetrate and cook the food through. Microwaves, on the other hand, penetrate into the food and cause heat to happen, so the food cooks all the way through more or less simultaneously, although the rate slows as the microwaves go deeper.

The rapidity of the rotation is according to the frequency. Only two frequency ranges are allocated to microwaves by the Federal Communications Commission and they cannot stray from these ranges because if they do they will interfere with radio communications. One is 890 to 940 megacycles, available only in the Americas but not used much, and the other is 2400 to 2500 megacycles, available world-wide. In a 2400-megacycle oven, the food molecules will rotate 2400 million times a second. Since a little power is used up on each successive layer of molecules, molecules deep inside the food rotate less than 180 degrees, so there is less heat, permitting a rare steak. Cooking does occur deep inside, but at a slower rate.

In an oven the microwaves are generated by a magnetron tube. They are channeled through a wave guide through a stirrer. The stirrer is a metal fan that adds the element of dispersion so the waves will more completely cover the oven cavity. These waves travel only in straight lines, therefore proper functioning depends on the stirrer and on the action of these waves bouncing off the metal sides of the oven.

Are microwave ovens dangerous?

They are dangerous in the same way that the hot sun in Texas is dangerous, or any other hot oven. Unfortunately there have been a lot of wild charges by doctors, bureaucrats, and elected officials that have been almost totally inadvised.

One medical administrator, for example, created a scare by warning that the microwaves could affect a heart Pacemaker. He neglected to mention (or perhaps he didn't know) that an ordinary pop-up toaster in the kitchen will also do this.

You and I walk through microwaves day and night, wherever there is radio, television, radar, and the sun itself. As with the sun, if microwave emission is too strong you feel the heat. Certainly, there is danger if you stay there and cook yourself. Unknowing children are fully protected by interlocks that must be built into the ovens.

The only factor to restrict use of this great appliance is cost. Most people who have tried it agree that it is more than worth it.

REFRIGERATORS: "OLD FAITHFUL" OF THE KITCHEN

There is probably no other manufactured product that gives as much for the consumer dollar as the refrigerator. It stays on duty every minute of every day and night, often for as long as 15 or 20 years, controlling its own temperature, recycling itself on and off, with very infrequent need for service.

It is such a great appliance that it is unfortunate that it is such a monstrosity. Refrigerators are very handsome per se, but they are too big and inflexible to really fit in with kitchen design. In many cases it's almost like parking your car in your kitchen. The car might be beautiful, but it just doesn't belong.

The best treatment for a refrigerator is to design it into a cabinet run and then use available trim kits to install cabinet paneling to match the cabinets, or plastic laminate to match the countertops, or even wallpaper or fabric. This raises the cost, but it helps integrate the design.

Mechanically, the refrigerator consists of a compressor, or pump, which pumps the refrigerant; an evaporator, or plate, which gets cold and cools the cabinet, and a condenser that transfers heat from the cabinet.

Basic features to be found on any model include shelving, crispers, ice cube trays, a freezing compartment, and light. Special features on better models would include rollers, a 7-day meat keeper, a butter conditioner, an ice maker, egg holders, and convertible doors.

ARE YOU ENERGY-CONSCIOUS?
NEW KITCHEN SAVES WATTS
AND DOLLARS

Should a patriotic American stop using the electric carving knife because of the energy crisis?

Some zealous Congressmen have suggested such measures, unaware probably that the total energy consumption and cost of an electric carving knife for an entire year comes to about 8 kilowatt hours, or 17 cents!

The fact is that nearly every improvement in kitchen appliances will save energy and money over the models of only a few years ago.

Refrigerators are better insulated, and the frost-free feature is less expensive than monthly defrosting by which you "throw away" all the cold in the old refrigerator and then run it to make everything cold again.

And the dishwasher installed in the home by the builder will nearly always be the cheapest model that runs full cycle for all loads, large or small. An upgraded, higher-priced dishwasher with multiple controls will save water, energy and money by running enough for the load it has, but no more. And its improved insulation will help cut costs on the most expensive appliance in the home, an electric water heater, which costs, on the average, $88 per year.

A microwave oven used for all feasible cooking jobs will save 75% in energy costs.

The accompanying table showing average wattage, consumption and cost for various home appliances shows annual figures. It is based on figures from the Electric Energy Association and calculated by the American Institute of Kitchen Dealers.

POWER CONSUMPTION BY APPLIANCES

	Average Wattage	Kilowatt Hours Consumed Annually	Annual Cost .021¢ per Kilowatt Hour
FOOD			
Blender	386	15	.32
Broiler	1,436	100	2.10
Carving Knife	92	8	.17
Coffee Maker	894	106	2.23
Deep Fryer	1,448	83	1.74
Dishwasher	1,201	363	7.62
Freezer (Frostless) 15 cu ft	440	1,761	36.98
Frying Pan	1,196	186	3.91
Mixer	127	13	.27
Oven, Microwave	1,500	300	6.30
Oven, Self-Cleaning	4,800	1,146	24.07
Range	8,200	1,175	24.68
Refrigerator (Frostless) 12 cu ft	321	1,217	25.56
Toaster	1,146	39	.82
Waffle Iron	1,116	22	.46
Waste Disposer	445	30	.63
LAUNDRY			
Clothes Dryer	4,856	993	20.85
Iron (hand)	1,008	144	3.02
Washing Machine	512	103	2.16
Water Heater (Standard)	2,475	4,219	88.60
COMFORT			
Air Conditioner (room)	1,566	1,389	29.17
Electric Blanket	177	147	3.09
Dehumidifier	257	377	7.92
Fan (rollaway)	171	138	2.90
Heater (portable)	1,322	176	3.70
Heating Pad	65	10	.21
Humidifier	177	163	3.42
HEALTH			
Hair Dryer	381	14	.29
Shaver	14	1.8	.04
Sun Lamp	279	16	.34
Toothbrush	7	0.5	.01
ENTERTAINMENT			
Radio	71	86	1.81
Radio-Record Player	109	109	2.29
T.V. (Black & White)	237	362	7.60
T.V. (Color)	332	502	10.54
HOUSEWARES			
Clock	2	17	.36
Floor Polisher	305	15	.32
Sewing Machine	75	11	.23
Vacuum Cleaner	630	46	.97

There are some deluxe models that also offer ice cubes and ice water through the door. This, of course, and any ice-maker model, also requires a cold water line. Some models are available that provide for later installation of an ice maker, a good feature for the builder who wants to cut his costs without totally precluding the convenience.

There are four types: The single door, the 2-door top-mount, the 2-door bottom-mount, and the side-by-side.

The *single door* model is the lowest priced, and a spring-type door inside gives access to a freezer compartment that will be 10 to 20 degrees above the desired 0 degrees. So it is not a true freezer.

All other models have two doors with a solid barrier between freezer and refrigerator. So the freezer will hold at 0 degrees while the fresh food compartment will maintain a temperature of between 37 to 40 degrees.

Top-mount models have the freezer above the regular food compartment, and bottom-mounts have the freezer below. *Side-by-sides* have gained fast popularity by eliminating all the bending and stooping, and their gains have been directly in proportion to losses for the bottom-mounts.

Refrigerators may be free-standing or built-in. The built-ins are best from a design viewpoint, and they usually have wood fronts to match the cabinets. They require a refrigerator cabinet, adding to the cost.

There also are many "compact" refrigerators, which might be free-standing or built-in. These usually are found in mobile homes, vacation homes, recreational vehicles, offices, motels, and apartments, but they also are fine for the home as a luxury touch—for the den, rec room, master bedroom, or even to store cold drinks for the kids by the outside door to keep them out of the kitchen traffic patterns.

Conventional refrigerators must be defrosted, usually about once a month. Automatic models have separate freezer and fresh food compartments, and the latter will defrost itself but the freezer must be defrosted about once a year. No-frost models have dual controls for the two compartments and neither compartment should ever need defrosting. This runs about a penny a day more in operating cost.

A separate freezer, which might be upright or chest type, is good for large families or families that like to cut the frequency of their shopping trips. It is good for the budget-conscious person because it permits economies such as buying a half a hog and a half a steer which a butcher would carve up into the appropriate cuts and package and label for storage in the home freezer.

But there must be a place to put a freezer. This should not be in the kitchen. The basement, utility room, or garage would be better, but fewer houses are being built with basements, and, on the average, houses are getting smaller. Space, then, could be a problem.

Where there is a separate freezer, there is no need to have more than a conventional refrigerator except as a luxury.

DISHWASHERS: CHEAP AT TWICE THE PRICE

Washing dishes is the easiest task in the home. It is just a simple matter of applying a little hot water and soap to a succession of plates and glasses, requiring no skill, strength, or concentration, and thus there is little need for an expensive appliance to do the job. Ask any husband.

Home Economist Retta Presby, however, struggled through massive calculations to determine that any average American who lives to the age of 70 will have consumed 150 head of cattle, 2400 chickens, 225 lambs, 26 sheep, 310 pigs, 26 acres of grain, and 59 acres of fruits and vegetables.

Multiply that by the number of people in the family and break it down to the number of plates, dishes, glasses, pots, pans, etc., it takes for individual servings, and communicate it to The Great American Husband. Now he is beginning to wonder about giving the best years of his wife to this senseless job.

Dishwashers are no longer luxuries, they are essentials. It is difficult to rent an apartment that does not have a dishwasher. Builders are including them in their new-home appliance packages. A housewife who gets used to one in her first apartment will never go back to the old method, nor should she.

Dishwashers can be top-loading or front-loading. Top-loaders are "portable," which means free-standing. Front-loaders are built-in or convertible. A convertible comes on wheels, but can be installed under the counter later when the consumer has more money or moves to what she considers her permanent home.

Standard width for a built-in is 24 inches. All other dimensions are standardized to fit under the standard kitchen countertop with the base cabinets. Cabinet

"Cook-n-Clean Center" by Modern Maid solves the space problem in another way. Center includes eye-level oven, a super-thin cooktop and dishwasher below.

Another dishwasher solution in kitchens with small space is this special General Electric model which will fit under a sink with a 6-inch bowl.

Water-powered dishwasher needs no electric connection, recesses into countertop. In kitchens where there isn't room for regular dishwasher installation, this can be a solution. It is made by Coronet Imperial of St. Louis.

While there are big differences in disposers, their method of operation is substantially the same. Here a cutaway shows interior of Waste King grinding mechanism.

manufacturers offer dishwasher fronts to match their cabinets, so they can be made to blend in with kitchen design.

Some manufacturers of related kitchen products have cooperated to make dishwashers feasible even for very small kitchens.

One sink manufacturer, for example, makes a special double-bowl sink with one bowl deep, the other shallow enough to fit over an undercounter dishwasher. Another manufacturer offers a matching family of cooktop, eye-level oven, vent hood and dishwasher below, so all four fit in 30 inches of space.

One manufacturer makes a different kind of dishwasher that can be sunk into a countertop, over a dead corner, for example. This product is water-powered and therefore needs no electrical hookup.

In operation, a dishwasher is more economical than most people think. In a normal full cycle of two washes and three rinses, the housewife hears the spraying and roiling of about 800 gallons of water. But actually only about 15 gallons of water are consumed, less than she would use when washing by hand. In a dishwasher the water is used, filtered and recirculated, over and over.

In her apartment, the housewife always has had the builder model, the economy model. She turned the knob and it did the job.

The lower-priced single-control dishwasher will do an excellent job. All the fancy pushbutton models will do a lot more, however. They do add to performance.

For example, one pushbutton might be for warming plates for dinner. Another might be for fragile dishes that aren't very dirty, giving gentler action with less water and detergent.

Still another would boost water temperature in the final rinse for greater sanitation. Other buttons would be for pots and pans, or to give dishes a quick rinse after which it automatically waits for her to get the other dishes loaded. And then, of course, there's the regular cycle, the equivalent of the single control on the economy model.

For effective dishwasher operation, water temperature must be between 140 and 160 degrees. The increasing impurities in and hardness of water have not been much of a problem because dishwasher detergents are formulated to cope with a wide range of water conditions. But in some areas of excessive water hardness, a water softener might be needed.

GARBAGE DISPOSAL—A REAL GRIND

Most of us in today's world have mental pictures of women, their noses wrinkled in distaste, emptying garbage from the sink into paper bags to be carried out to a garbage can.

Those mental pictures are justification enough for the modern garbage disposer, an appliance that takes a small bite of electricity, a long drink of water, and then chews up all the garbage you feed it into tiny particles that wash down the drain with the waste water.

There are two types of disposers.

The batch-fed type has a locking cover that also serves as a switch. To operate this type you fill it with waste (just put it in, don't pack it in), lock the cover in place, and the disposer operates.

The continuous-feed type has a separate switch, usually on the wall over the sink. To operate this type the water is turned on, the switch turned on, and food waste is simply fed in until it all is gone.

Both must be operated with running cold water. Both will do the job with the same efficiency. Neither has any advantage over the other. It is a matter of personal preference.

There is, however, another way to categorize disposers, and this way the difference is vast.

There are cheap ones and there are expensive ones.

Buying a cheap disposer is like buying a cheap parachute. It is made of different materials that won't wear nearly as long, performance will not be as good, noise will be worse, and you will be lucky to get more than two or three years of use out of it.

Differences in quality are apparent in the fact that a good disposer will cost three times as much as the cheaper models. But the good one will be dependable for 10 years, it will install more easily, it will operate more quietly and it will do more.

Anyone who has had an unhappy experience with a disposer in the past should be aware of those big differences. Disposers that builders put into housing developments almost always are bought on a price basis, and that means the consumer gets a cheap disposer. You should be aware also that these "economy" disposers are made by the same manufacturers who make the very finest, so don't condemn a good brand name just because you got stuck with one of their cheapies 10 years ago.

Good disposers will dispose of bones, and fruit pits, and corn cobs, and some will even take normal household quantities of paper napkins and towels. They have trouble with food wastes that are particularly fibrous, such as corn husks or avocado leaves. They will handle these, but it will take longer because of the stringiness, so often it is easier to dispose of such waste with other kitchen trash. Celery and coffee grounds are no problem.

Metal should never be dropped in a disposer, not even small bits like the staples on tea bags.

There was a time when disposer repairmen would drop glass pop bottles into an operating disposer to clean it. This was a good way to clean the disposer, but the glass particles would collect in the plumbing lines, catch food particles and eventually clog the lines. Therefore, glass is not recommended. Bones and fruit pits will do the same cleaning job.

Incidentally, there are about 100 cities in the U.S. that require, by ordinance, disposers in all new residential construction. These cities benefit from improved sanitation and from considerable economies in garbage collection.

And, for those who are not in cities, any septic tank system which meets HUD Minimum Property Standards can handle the slight added load from a disposer.

VENTILATING HOODS—FOR INDOORS ECOLOGY

A ventilating hood provides the gift of fresh air in the kitchen. It stops airborne cooking odors at their source, traps grease and soil that otherwise would end up on walls, ceilings and draperies, and should be considered one of the essentials over every cooking appliance. That means over both the cooktop and wall ovens when these are built-in, over both the cooking surface and the oven in an eye-level range, and over either a microwave oven or barbecue grill when these are present in the kitchen.

There are many things you should know about vent-hoods that affect their performance. There are different types, and performance features, and they must be powered in relation to their distance above the cooking appliance. All vent hoods manufactured by members of the Home Ventilating Institute have performance ratings, and they also have sone ratings that measure their noise levels.

As for types, there are ductless and ducted vent hoods.

Ventilating hoods have become decorative as well as functional. These, the Chuck Wagon series by Broan, have various optional straps and plaques that apply with adhesive and can be changed. These take big dual squirrel cage blower rated for cfm and sones—air movement and sound level. They have solid state controls for light and power.

Ducted types are better. They filter the air as it enters the hood, and then they have ductwork to exhaust it to the outside. Because of the ductwork, their fan units can be remote, out of the kitchen, to minimize noise, and they can have more powerful fan units for greater air movement.

But there are some places where ducted hoods are not practical; in apartments, for example. Here a non-ducted hood is much better than none. These have excellent filter systems that gather the air, clean it and then exhaust it back into the kitchen, commonly from vents in the top that direct it upward. Thus the heat and moisture of cooking is exhausted back into the kitchen rather than being vented to the outside, but grease and odor have been removed.

Some expensive wall ovens are made with attached vent hoods. These are designed to match the ovens. They pull out to protrude a few inches when in operation during cooking, then can be pushed in to fit flush with the oven at other times.

Hoods come in many shapes, colors, and sizes. Some are squared, some angled, some curved. They come in colors to match major appliance colors—mainly the earth colors, such as avocado and harvest—or in white, chrome, or other options.

Some are manufactured with three finished sides

to project over kitchen peninsulas, or with four finished sides for kitchen islands. One brand has modular sections so it can be made larger or smaller on-site. While most are made of steel, at least one brand is constructed of fiber glass.

In addition, most cabinet manufacturers offer custom hoods of wood to match the cabinets, and most kitchen dealers have local sheet-metal sources for making custom hoods.

The perfect vent hood in one kitchen might be unsatisfactory in another kitchen because the layout of the kitchen can affect the performance of the product. For example, a certain cfm rating in a hood over a built-in cooktop that is installed against a wall might be inadequate over a cooktop installed in a peninsula or island, because of cross-drafts in the kitchen. Added duct run from a peninsula also would require greater power.

In order of importance, there are these four considerations in selecting a vent hood:

1) *Be sure of enough power.* A hood must take out smoke, odors and grease as fast as they are produced, and it must have power to overcome the resisting pressure of the length of duct run with its elbows and end caps. Look first for a Home Ventilating Institute rating. Otherwise, be wary of suspiciously low prices for any power rating.
2) Then consider *noise level.* Again, check HVI sone ratings.
3) Select the right product then on the basis of *style, service,* and *workmanship.*
4) Then consider *price.* There will still be price variations, big ones, even after the first three considerations, but to put price ahead of those other considerations would be a disservice to the housewife who must live with the product.

As for performance, the FHA and the HVI both require a minimum of 40 cfm per foot of hood length. So a 140-cfm fan would be minimum for a 42-inch hood. Most of these are fan type and have retail prices well under $50, but this type is for minimum performance.

For fair performance, a 200-cfm fan could qualify, but it would not get the job done when the cook is using all burners or cooking something exceptionally smoky. Fan type vent-hoods in this range still usually retail for about $50 or less but might be noisy. A centrifugal blower would be more quiet for only about $5 or $10 more.

For good performance, think in terms of 300 cfm and up. These will have several speeds, or with solid state control an infinite range of speeds. You will seldom see a fan-type here. Most will have twin centrifugal blowers (often called "squirrel cage") which will be quiet and might sell at retail for as low as $75 or up to twice that.

In tightly constructed houses, a window might have to be opened slightly to permit a vent hood to do its job. A hood should be 24 inches to 30 inches over the range.

LITTLE EXTRAS FOR BIG DIFFERENCES

The appliances described so far are the routine equipment that might be found in any new kitchen. There might be extra margins of quality—the extra features interpretable into extra convenience or extra function—but still, they are basics.

There are many other appliances that can be built in and that can add up to a super kitchen.

When a housewife moves into her new home, for example, she must go out and buy a toaster, and an electric mixer, blender, and perhaps a knife sharpener. She will go to a housewares department and look for some sort of box that her husband can hang on a wall or attach under a wall cabinet to dispense her foil and plastic wrap and paper towels.

Whatever she buys, she has to find space for the item, both in use and when she wants to put it away. She has a shining new kitchen, but every time she buys something for it she finds she has bought a problem.

It doesn't have to be that way. All of these items can be designed into the kitchen in the first place. No storage problem. No countertop space problem. Here are a few examples.

Built-in toasters are available. They can be wired and recessed into the wall, tilting out for use and then pushing back to their flush position.

Two different manufacturers offer two different built-in mixing systems, combining all mixing, blending, juicing, and other such functions. In both of these, the motor is mounted under the counter, which helps minimize noise, and all attachments go in a base cabinet directly under the appliance, at the point of

Infra-red heating lamps are incorporated in this Trade Wind hood, so it serves as a food warmer while it vents.

And ventilating fans aren't what they used to be, as these pictures prove. The ceiling model is by Emerson. The wall model is by NuTone. They suck in air around the perimeter. All of these fans and hoods have HVI power and sone ratings.

Another built-in appliance that helps organize kitchen and eliminate problems is the built-in mixing center. The two shown here are by Ronson (above) and NuTone (below). Both take full range of attachments, and storage of all these and bowls is right at point of use.

use. In one of these systems only a small stainless steel plate shows above the counter, and when lifted it exposes the drive shaft onto which all attachments fit. The other system has a small control panel that protrudes above the counter.

There also are built-in can-openers, electric-powered, that recess into the wall, and built-in knife-sharpeners.

There are either electric or hydronic heating units engineered to recess into the kick-space under a base cabinet.

There are different types of food-warming appliances. One is a slide-out drawer, similar to those used in restaurants but designed for the modern residential kitchen. Wood trim kits are available for these so they accept paneling to match the cabinets. Another food warmer is a wired rectangular glass-ceramic plate that recesses into the countertop. This has the added advantage of providing a place to put hot pans from the cooktop. Other food warmers use infra-red radiation and mount under the wall cabinets, and one ventilating hood incorporates this warming feature.

There are water purification systems that become more relevant in these days of bottled drinking water. One can be mounted on the wall or recessed into the wall near the sink, or mounted on a wall cabinet near the sink. These need a cold water line, of course. There are several others in the developmental stage.

There are musical-intercom systems that can put music throughout the house from a master panel in the kitchen, which also monitor other rooms (such as the baby's bedroom) and incorporate burglar and fire alarms.

Paper caddies can be recessed into the wall. Automatic ice-makers are available and can be free-standing or can be built-in under the counter. There are also instant hot water dispensers.

Trash compactors can be free-standing or they can replace a 15-inch base cabinet under the counter. They require a 3-wire line, and should take a separate 15-amp fuse. But there are a dozen different brands, so specifications will vary and might be changed.

5

Sinks and the Counter-Revolution

Kitchen countertops are playing an increasingly important role in the modern kitchen. Years ago when the sink was recessed in the only countertop in the kitchen, they were called sinktops. Gradually, new materials and new ideas changed this ordinary part of the kitchen. In the middle 1950s, high-pressure plastic laminates were popular as a surfacing for these countertops, but it was difficult to mate sink with sinktop in a way that would prevent moisture seepage and consequent rotting. To answer that challenge a clamp-down rim, the "Hudee" rim, was developed.

At around the same time the technique known as postforming became popular. This is the technique that gives a clean seamless sweep of plastic surface from the front of the countertop to the back, curving up at the back to cover a 4-inch backsplash or more.

And then sink manufacturers started wondering why sinks had to be so ordinary. They started improving their surfaces and materials. They added lights and soap dispensers. They became innovative in configurations.

All of these factors led to the counter-revolution. Sinks and countertops became things of beauty and previously-undreamed-of function. They became parts of the new kitchen concept.

In more recent years, new adhesives and sealants have led to a return of the "self-rimming" sink that does not require a Hudee-type rim. Now either type can be trusted for long years of use.

The most popular sink is of stainless steel. The most inexpensive is made of porcelain-on-steel, often called pressed steel. A more expensive type is porcelained cast iron. The newest material is molded plastic, or artificial marble, commonly used for bathrooms but not kitchens.

Both porcelain-on-steel and cast iron sinks now come in glamour colors and with innovative configurations. But the former can chip easily. The latter is very durable but more expensive.

Stainless steel costs more than either, but its prices vary according to gauge of the steel and nickel and chrome content. Some are shiny, some are not.

All of these differences are more or less academic in new homes where the sink is provided by the builder. The kitchen sink, after all, is a small part of a kitchen and most housewives will accept anything the builder provides.

But the differences are significant in custom homes and in kitchen remodeling, where the housewife is shown the options for added beauty and utility. In stainless steel, she will have a definite preference for either the satin or brilliant finish, and she should be given the opportunity to choose. She might want the bright color of a porcelain finish, or the futuristic design of a particular brand. She might want a deluxe model with three compartments, a fluorescent light attached, soap and lotion dispensers, a separate pull-out spray, a purification device for the drinking water, an instant hot water device for instant soups and beverages, and built-in compartments for ice or for placement of a built-in small appliance.

The new designer styling has pretty much done away with standard measurements in kitchen sinks. Most still are 21 or 22 inches from front to back because the depth of the countertop is standardized, and the bowl itself usually is 16 inches from front to back. But these dimensions vary according to brand and style.

While the usual depth of the bowl is 7-1/2 inches, this too can vary widely. For example, a triple-bowl

Decorator colors characterize sinks of porcelain-on-steel or cast iron. This cast iron model by Kohler is the Trieste, with two big working bowls and one in the center to take the disposer.

Kohler's Urbanite is unique in that it combines a disposer compartment in a single bowl sink to meet space limitations. It's only 25×22".

How classy a kitchen sink can be is proven by this, the self-rimming stainless steel "Cuisine Classique" by Elkay. With the glamorous name go glamorous functions, even to a color-coded temperature control. Back ledge features, from left, include: Separate goose-neck faucet for disposer compartment; pull-out spray; single main faucet; water supply knob; color-coded temperature-control knob (from blue to red, for cold to hot), and then another goose-neck faucet for vegetable-cleaning compartment.

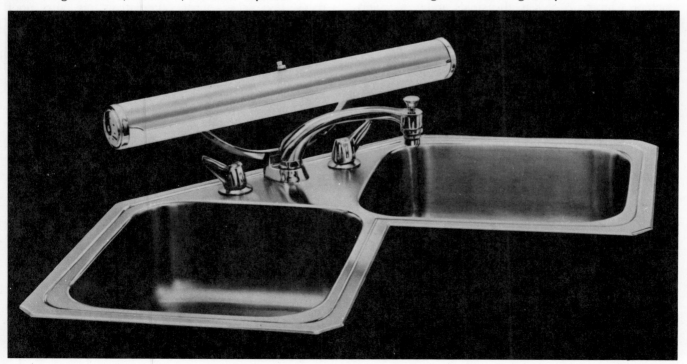

Another example is pie-cut for corner installation and with a fluorescent fixture mounted behind the faucet. This also is by Elkay.

sink might have a small vegetable sink between two larger bowls, and this might be only 3-1/2 inches deep. It also might be round, and it might be the ideal place for the disposer. A 3-1/2-inch depth for one bowl of a double-bowl sink allows the housewife to sit while cleaning or preparing vegetables and salads.

While there are many round and oval sinks, they normally are used in bathrooms or hospitality areas rather than in the kitchen.

For corner installation, sink manufacturers offer double-bowl sinks in a pie-cut configuration. For kitchens where space is at a premium, there also are special depths (5-1/2 inches) to permit one bowl to fit over a built-in dishwasher.

Sinks may come with faucets and other attachments, or simply with punched holes so faucets can be purchased separately.

In the latter case, options are limited by the number of holes punched. But it will always be possible to accommodate either the traditional pair of faucets—hot and cold—or the more modern single-handle faucet.

A single-bowl sink is adequate if the kitchen is equipped with a dishwasher. Even with a dishwasher, the double-bowl is desirable.

Stainless steel sinks come in 18-gauge and 20-gauge. The 18-gauge is heavier and much more satisfactory. Two other figures that require interpretation refer to the mix of the alloys. For example, 18-8 would mean 18 percent chrome content and 8 percent nickel content. Chrome relates to the sink's ability to stand up and keep its finish over the years. Nickel gives the steel the ability to withstand corrosion.

There are three basic surfaces for kitchen countertops.

The standard utility surface is decorative high-pressure plastic laminate, such as the well-known Formica. It should be 1/16-inch thick for horizontal applications in the kitchen. The thinner 1/32-inch vertical grade material is not recommended, although it often is used as a cost-cutting measure.

The other two basic materials are for use in conjunction with high-pressure laminates. One is laminated hardwood, the familiar "butcher block," for cutting operations. The other is tempered glass ceramic (or ceramic tile, stainless steel, or marble) used as a counter insert for hot pans direct from the range, or for cutting.

This is not to say that all, nor even that most, kitchens actually have these three types of surfaces.

Most have only the plastic laminate surfacing.

And as a consequence, the woman who must take a hot pan from the oven and put it down quickly must put it in the sink, or on the range top if there is a space there. And she cuts bread or meats or vegetables on the plastic laminate and, in the course of only a couple of years, puts thousands of tiny cuts in it. If, in an emergency, she puts a hot pan down on the unprotected countertop, permanent damage can result. Then the top must be replaced, or a kitchen specialist or top fabricator can cut out the damaged part and replace it with the counter insert that should have been there in the first place.

In the far west, ceramic tile is widely used for the entire kitchen countertop. This is an excellent and beautiful material. But it also is much noisier, its hard surface dulls knives, and dishes break more easily on it. The same is true of marble and of the newer artificial marbles so widely used as bathroom vanity tops. Stainless steel is a good material, but it can be dented, it dulls knives, and the scratches and stains on this surface are difficult to remove.

Many kitchen designers will plan whole sections of laminated wood into the countertop, along with a glass ceramic section or insert. Many like to include custom stainless steel sinks in the design with stainless steel drainboards or extensions for the hot pan problem.

Forget linoleum. It went out with running boards and rumble seats. Vinyls, low-pressure polyester laminates, and other plastic alternatives are also poor choices. They are fine for vertical surfaces and good for table tops, but not for kitchen counters.

Since high pressure plastic laminated tops are the standard, from this point on we'll simply call them tops. Two types of tops can be identified: self-edged and postformed. Self-edged tops are flat. They have a square front and the edging is a separate piece of the same material, hence the term self-edged. The backsplash is a separate piece with a square inside corner, but firmly attached at the shop before delivery.

The backsplash can be any height, but the standard is 4 inches. The usual alternative is a backsplash that rises all the way to the bottoms of the wall cabinets, adding much to the overall cleanability of the kitchen. This high backsplash is seldom done with postformed tops because of equipment limitations.

Postformed tops present one clean sweep of plastic surface from the bottom of the front edge to the top of the backsplash.

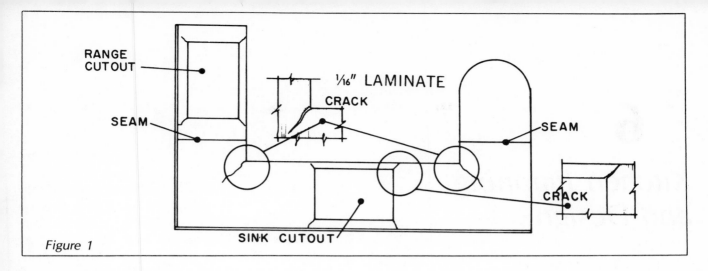

Figure 1

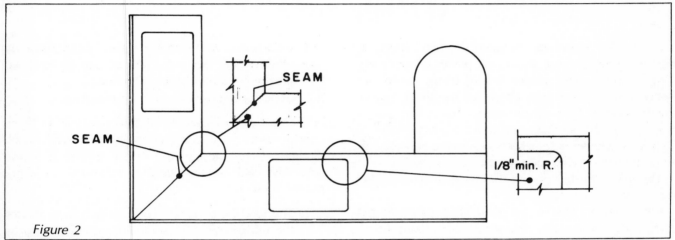

Figure 2

Improper placing of laminate seams can cause cracks. When seam is mitered from front to back corner it avoids stresses that come with no miter. Figure 1 shows wrong way, Figure 2 shows right way. All corners of sink or range cutouts should be radiused. Square corners in these places tend to crack. Formica Corp.

Fabricators usually use 3/4-inch particleboard as a corestock. The finished product must be at least that thickness, and it might vary up to 1-3/4 inches. But there would have to be some special reason for the latter thickness. In normal use it would be sheer extravagance. Depth of the top from front to rear would be 24 inches or 25 inches, enough to extend a minimum of 1/8 inch or a maximum of 1/2 inch over the cabinets beneath. These figures are from the standards of the National Association of Plastic Fabricators.

Regular kitchen countertops, properly attached to the base cabinets, need no backing sheet for dimensional stability. The structure itself will prevent warping.

But peninsulas that extend several feet out from the base cabinets must have backing sheets.

Tops that must be positioned tightly between walls must be 1/4-inch to 3/8-inch short. A top that measures the same as the between-walls dimension will not go into position.

Out-of-square walls are always a problem. Theoretically, every wall meets another wall at 90 degrees. In practice it just doesn't happen. So, in practice, tops often must be slightly out-of-square.

The rule-of-thumb used by kitchen specialists on corner squareness is a simple formula: 3 ft. + 4 ft. = 5 ft.

To use it, measure the base wall to a point 3 feet from the corner and mark the point. Then measure along the side wall and mark a point 4 feet from the corner. Now measure the direct distance, point to point. It should be 5 feet.

If it measures less than 5 feet, the side wall is coming in. If it measures more than 5 feet, the side wall is going out.

Communicate the precise measurements to the top fabricator and he can allow for it so that the top will fit.

6

Kitchen Planning and Design

The primary ingredient in good kitchen design is common sense. You've got to have places to put things. You've got to have places to put things down. It's better to store things near where you use them. You've got to have a little elbow room. And when you're working in the kitchen you don't want to have to step aside whenever somebody else in the house wants to go from the living room to the bathroom.

Those are the basics, but they raise several loaded questions.

For example, you've got to have a place to put things. But how many things? A 2-bedroom house presumes a family of two or three, maybe four. A 4-bedroom house presumes a family of five or six. Obviously a homeowner needs a lot more pots and pans and dishes and space for a family of six than for a family of two.

The concepts of "enough room" and "good kitchen layout" are matters of opinion for most people until they actually start storing foods and dishes and working in a kitchen. Kitchen experts through the years have formularized most kitchen planning principles to remove the subjective guesses and substitute objective facts and measurements that always will work.

The considerations are these:

1. Storage space that is both ample and logical. Ample means enough, but not too much. Too much would be wasteful both of money and of floorspace in the home. Logical means having enough storage space at the proper places.
2. Countertop space that is both ample and in the right places.
3. Well-planned placement and areas for each of the major appliances and their related activities.

4. Reduction of waste motion. (Few of us are naturally efficient, but our inefficiencies can be lessened greatly by good kitchen planning.)
5. Good lighting and good color-matching.

The best way to start planning to satisfy all of those considerations is to consider the activity areas. Each of these relates closely to a major appliance or the sink. And each requires its own cabinetry and work space. These are:

1. The food preparation center, which incorporates the refrigerator. This sometimes is referred to as the mixing center.
2. The cooking and serving center, which includes the range or, in built-in installations, at least the cooktop.
3. The clean-up center, which incorporates the sink. Major appliances found in this area include the dishwasher and disposer.

Many housewives also want an eating area in the kitchen, and there is a growing trend to include a planning center which serves as the housewife's "office." Such a planning center will include at least a desktop with some storage facility for household bills, notes and the like. Well-planned ones will also include a telephone and an intercom which provides communication throughout the house, monitoring of baby's sleeping or play areas, and even burglar and fire alarms.

Other possible centers could include a bar, a hobby center, or sewing center, but these are functions of space.

The ground rule for arranging these three major centers is to form a triangle, and the straight-line distance

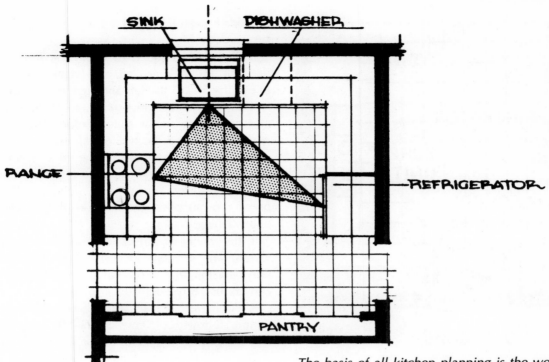

SINK DISHWASHER

RANGE

REFRIGERATOR

PANTRY

The basis of all kitchen planning is the work triangle. It connects the food preparation center, which includes the refrigerator; cooking center, which includes the range; and the cleanup center with the sink and dishwasher. Total distance from middle front of sink, to range to refrigerator and back to sink, should be from 12 to 22 feet. Within these limits the housewife has sufficient freedom of action but doesn't have to cover tiring distances.

between the front center of the sink, refrigerator and cooktop must not total more than 22 feet nor less than 12 feet.

That is called the work triangle, and it is the basis for all kitchen planning.

The distance from the sink to the refrigerator should be from 4 to 7 feet; from sink to range, 4 to 6 feet, and between range and refrigerator, 4 to 9 feet.

Any one-piece range fits into that triangle. A built-in installation, however, adds a fourth element, since there is a separate oven and cooktop. The guideline here is to put the oven outside the triangle since it is used least, although it often can be designed within the triangle.

Both the maximum (22 feet) and the minimum (12 feet) of the work triangle are important. More than 22 feet wastes steps, energy, and time. Less than 12 feet crowds the appliances and activities too close together.

Kitchen planning starts with the sink. A kitchen designer always locates it first, partially because good planning usually centers it with refrigerator to the right of it, or clockwise from it, and the cooking and serving area to the left of it, or counter-clockwise. In addition, the sink must go where the plumbing lines are, and location of the plumbing lines usually is determined by other factors, such as location of bathrooms.

The sink is the center of clean-up activity before as well as after the meal. So plenty of counter space is required.

There should be 36 inches of counter space to the right of the sink, and there should be 30 inches of counter space to the left.

The dishwasher should be adjacent to the sink. If a dishwasher is not included, a 24-inch cabinet should be designed adjacent to the sink for later installation of a dishwasher.

If a dishwasher is not included, a double-bowl sink

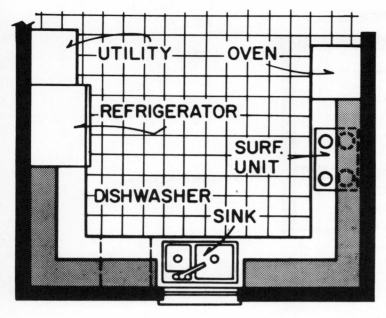

U Shaped

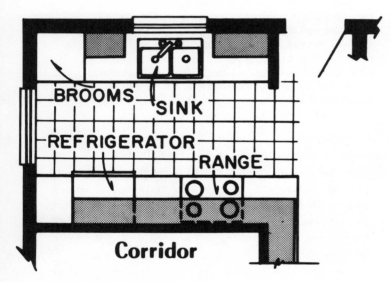

Corridor

The four basic kitchen configurations are the U shape, the L shape, the Corridor, and the One Wall. The U and the L usually afford efficient work triangles without cross traffic. A U or L broken by a door cuts efficiency by permitting cross traffic. The corridor is efficient if it is a closed corridor. If it is open, traffic cuts through. A central island or a peninsula often is used to help form the work triangle.

is needed. Even if there is a dishwasher, a double-bowl sink is desirable.

If fillers are required to make the run of cabinets fit flush to walls to left and right, the best place to put them is to the left and right of the sink cabinet.

Many kitchen activities relate closely to both refrigerator and range so, as stated before, the sink is best placed between those two other centers.

Storage must be provided near the sink for clean-up supplies, for fruits and vegetables that do not require refrigeration, for sauce pans, coffee pot and food preparation supplies, and for foods that require soaking and washing.

If the recommended counter space to the right (36 inches) and left (30 inches) of the sink cannot be provided, the absolute minimums would be 24 inches and 18 inches respectively.

A double-bowl sink with one shallow bowl will permit sit-down convenience for the housewife when she is cleaning vegetables or for similar tasks.

The sink does not have to go under a window. This is a matter of personal preference, and the idea that it enabled the mother to watch the kids playing has always been questionable. At best, it leaves a lot of gaps in the surveillance. If there is one window, it might be best to save it for a breakfast-lunch area.

We have referred to the area around the refrigerator as the food preparation area, or the mixing center. Some kitchen designers separate these in different ways, but the functions and needs are closely related.

It is good to localize various types of food storage here—cold foods in the refrigerator and its freezer compartment, canned goods in a pantry unit of some sort. Pantry units can be obtained 84 inches high or as wall or base cabinets, with fold-out vertical racks to hold a maximum number of cans, or with revolving shelves that are particularly good for corners.

The refrigerator door must open into the work triangle, not away from it. And there must be at least 18 inches of landing space where the refrigerator door opens. Side-by-side refrigerator-freezers tend to defeat this principle, but with these models it is the refrigerator door, not the freezer door, that should open to the landing space.

When the food preparation and mixing functions are included in this activity center, there should be 36 to 42 inches of counter space on the door-opening side of the refrigerator.

A maple insert in the countertop is particularly useful here. It could be as small as 12 inches wide, or it could be a whole section of countertop. Women use knives often when preparing food and it is next to impossible to keep from cutting the countertop.

The maple cutting board also can be a pull-out accessory of the base cabinet, positioned over a drawer.

Here, also, is the place for a built-in mixer, with a cabinet below for its many accessories.

The cooking center is the most active area of the kitchen after the sink and cleanup center.

The built-in cooktop should have at least 18 inches of counter space on each side.

A built-in oven needs 24 inches of counter space.

A one-piece range needs at least the minimum 18 inches on each side, but it is much better to provide at least 24 inches on the inside of the work triangle.

Provide a counter insert of either stainless steel or glass ceramic near the range for placing hot pans. The plastic laminate of a countertop should never be subjected to heat over 270 degrees.

Since the oven is the least-used appliance in the kitchen, built-in installations can be out of the work triangle. However, it still will need its counter space.

In their specifications for every model, manufacturers of built-in ovens always list a height above the floor for the bottom of the oven cut-out.

A woman can work with least effort at an oven if the opened door is 3 to 4 inches below her elbow level. The usable range here is from 1 to 7 inches below elbow level. If there is a choice, relate the height of the opened oven door to the user's elbow level.

The cooktop usually will be 36 inches from the floor because it is cut into the countertop and that's the height of the counter. It could be dropped as much as 4 inches, and a lot of housewives would probably appreciate it.

Because both the built-in wall oven and the refrigerator are high appliances, a common design error is to put them together. This should never be done, because both need their own landing space. It does not help to have a landing space on either side when these two are together because that non-solution would put the landing space on the wrong side for either the refrigerator or the oven.

If the range corner of the work triangle is oriented

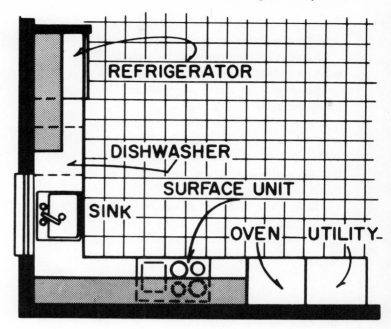

L Shaped

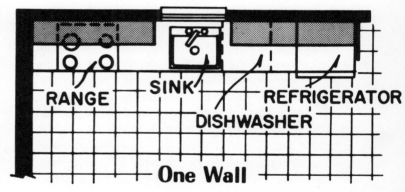

One Wall

toward the dining area, it might be combined with a serving center. This is common, although the serving center need not be in conjunction with any particular appliance.

The serving center needs storage space for the toaster, serving trays, ready-to-eat foods, platters, serving dishes, table linens, and napkins. There should be at least 30 inches of counter space.

Needless to say, the serving center should be near and accessible to the eating area. Since this is where the china and glassware are stored for serving and eating, it also can be considered as a china center.

Families like eating space in the kitchen, supplementary to a separate dining area, and most builders provide this space in most of their homes.

This adds another center to be included in the kitchen plan—the eating center.

This might be along a peninsula, an island, or it might protrude from a wall.

If it is a peninsula, island, or protrusion, allow at least 42 inches clearances from its end to the opposite wall. Do not put the refrigerator or wall oven on that opposite wall where an open door would block traffic.

Allow 24 inches of elbow room for each place for the lunchers.

For breakfast, the minimum depth should be at least 15 inches. For dinner, it should be 24 inches.

A table and chairs require at least 8×6-1/2 feet.

Tables and chairs are simpler and easier. Islands and peninsulas add much to the impact of the kitchen, and they are not complicated.

If an eat-on peninsula is to be included, a run of 14 feet, at least, is needed for the wall from which it protrudes. This allows a minimum of eight feet for the kitchen, including the 24-inch-wide peninsula, and six feet for the dining area.

The peninsula is different only in that it is connected to the cabinets along the wall, extending out into the room to add design interest, give extra storage and counter space, and keep traffic out of the work triangle.

With an additional expenditure, a homeowner can have an island with a maple block top that can serve as a food mixing and preparation center on one side, a snack bar on the other. At relatively little more cost, he can make this a beautifully textured brick island, then add a built-in barbecue unit and a cooktop.

If the opposite side of the peninsula will provide a snack bar instead of a dining area, the 6 feet can be reduced. There must be at least 30 inches from the edge of the snack bar to the wall for seating, and this is a bit tight.

Standard height for island or peninsula would be 36 inches. The snack bar height would drop to 30 inches. If the snack bar is not dropped, high chairs or stools would be needed.

If the snack bar is 36 inches high, the top will have to be extended from 12 to 18 inches for knee space, depending on the type of seating.

If, however, the snack bar is dropped to 30 inches, the minimum for knee space is 15 inches.

The island or peninsula also can be an excellent place for the sink and clean-up center. Unfortunately, this usually will add to plumbing expense.

If possible, the kitchen should be laid out so there will be no traffic crossing any legs of the work triangle. This will not always be possible, but if compromises must be made, the range center should be kept most sacrosanct.

Avoid placing the refrigerator too close to an adjoining wall. If the door cannot be opened far enough, the crisper trays cannot be removed for cleaning.

As a rule of thumb, the kitchen should have at least 10 feet (linear) of base cabinets and 10 feet of wall cabinets. These are absolute minimums.

Allow 27 inches of space along both walls to turn a corner. A base corner filler is the most economical way to turn the corner but gives only dead space. This insures full operation of adjacent doors and drawers.

Other better ways to turn a corner are (1) with corner units that give reach-in storage space; (2) with a lazy susan cabinet that makes all the corner space easily accessible, and which requires 36 inches along each wall; (3) with a sink or appliance cutting the corner on the diagonal, requiring varying amounts of wall space.

For turning a corner above the counter, a wall corner filler (with dead space, so not desirable) takes 15 inches along each wall. Diagonal wall cabinets can be used, or open diagonal shelving, or butted wall cabinets that have reach-in space. A diagonal wall cabinet takes 24 inches along each wall.

In the home-planning stage, the kitchen should be planned before house plans are finalized. Otherwise it can be costly to the kitchen. For example, a door placed in a corner of the kitchen must use both walls of that corner, with a resultant loss of 30 inches of valuable kitchen space. If this door is installed at least 30 inches from the corner, cabinets can be run all the way to the corner and the only loss is the dimension of the door itself, and its framing. And windows should be a minimum of 12-3/4 inches from a corner for the same reason.

In any inside corner of a cabinet installation, watch for clearances. Normally there will be doors and drawers along both sides of the corner. If they are butted precisely, there might not be clearance for the knob or pull. This would call for a filler to create the clearance. Minimum for clearance is 1/2 inch.

When blank base cabinets are used to turn a corner, the blank end of the cabinet does not have to fill the entire space where it is not exposed. In fact, it is better if it does not fill the space because it is very difficult to reach into such a corner and much of the space would, therefore, be wasted.

Diagonal corner cabinets can add much interest to the kitchen design. However, they use up a lot of wall space. For example, a cabinet that has 20 inches of exposed surface along the diagonal requires 39 inches along each wall. A 30-inch diagonal cabinet requires 45-1/2 inches along each wall. (This presumes that the depth of adjacent cabinets is 24-1/2 inches.) This does not waste any space, because all space inside the diagonal cabinet is usable. But it uses wall space that, depending on overall kitchen dimensions, might be needed for other purposes.

For the above reason, kitchen specialists usually advise that no sink or appliance over 32 inches in width be used to turn a corner diagonally.

In a straight-wall assembly, the distance from the front edge of the countertop to the front edge of the sink is usually 2 inches. In a diagonal assembly, this distance must be increased to 3 inches so as not to intrude into adjoining cabinet area on each side.

Conventional cabinets can be positioned diagonally across corners. But this creates big pie-shaped dead spaces on either side, wasting kitchen space.

Putting it all together makes the kitchen—the cabinets, the appliances, the corners, the work centers, the activity areas—with the basic work triangle measuring from 12 feet to 22 feet.

This results in one of four basic configurations, or "kinds" of kitchens.

These are the one-wall kitchen, sometimes called straight-line; the corridor kitchen, sometimes called two-wall or pullman or parallel; the L-shaped kitchen which turns one corner, and the U-shaped kitchen which has two inside corners.

All of these have variations. If, for example, a door interrupts the continuity of an L or a U kitchen, it becomes a broken L, or a broken U. If an island or a peninsula is used to achieve the work triangle, it might be called an island kitchen or a peninsula kitchen.

In the one-wall kitchen, the work centers and the appliances are arranged along one wall. This means,

of course, that there is no work triangle, and usually both storage space and counter space are much too limited for efficiency or convenience. It is, however, the most economical kind of kitchen, and the most easily installed.

For vacation homes, offices and the like, this configuration is available from about a dozen manufacturers in one manufactured piece, usually called a unit kitchen, or a compact kitchen.

A complete unit kitchen will include a sink, two surface burners (or more), and, underneath, an oven compartment and a refrigerator compartment.

A corridor kitchen adds the opposite wall, making possible a tight, efficient work triangle and added usable storage and counter space. Where the opposite wall is too distant, a peninsula or island can be added to create one side of a corridor kitchen, and in this case at least one of the work centers will be placed in the created counter space.

The only disadvantage of a corridor kitchen is that through traffic always cuts through two legs of the work triangle. In a family with active children this can be bothersome.

The L-shaped kitchen is the most popular, affords the most efficient work triangle, and is never bothered with through traffic. While the two sides of the L are usually along two walls of the room, in larger kitchens one leg of the L often is formed with a peninsula that affords a snack bar on the other side, outside the work area.

A U-shaped kitchen, as its name indicates, has three sides. Customarily these are three of the walls of the room, but often a peninsula is added to make a U out of what otherwise would be an L. The objective of a U-shape is to place a work area in each side, making a well-balanced equilateral work triangle.

U-shaped kitchens usually go into fairly good-sized rooms, but sometimes there is an effort to squeeze one into dimensions that are too tight. The base wall, or middle leg, of the U must be at least 9 feet to give the desirable 5 feet clearance in the middle after the cabinets are in.

Broken U's or L's are signs of failure in the house design. They happen when a door has been placed without allowing for the kitchen design. Kitchen design still can be good except for the basic flaw of interrupted work from cross traffic. Traffic through the kitchen always will cross two legs of the work triangle.

As noted previously, islands and peninsulas can be used to form the work triangle, provide eating space in the kitchen, or added counter for work space.

Sometimes a peninsular eating area is nothing more than a countertop projecting from a cabinet line or a wall, with a supporting leg at the far end. These can be square, rectangular, kidney-shaped, free-form or in any shape desired. This is a simple, easy installation that, in effect, makes the dinette table a structural part of the house and relieves the home-owner of the need to buy a dinette.

Other peninsulas that also provide storage space are a bit more involved. Projecting from the cabinet line, they will consist of regular base cabinets, a counter which might also hold the sink or cooktop, and a line of wall cabinets overhead which would house the vent hood.

Both wall and base cabinets in such a peninsula can be ordered to open on either side of the peninsula, or on both sides. When they open on both sides it adds greatly to convenience, because then dishes or other items can be stored or removed from either side.

Here are a few pointers for these peninsulas.

The base cabinet at the end of the peninsula should have a kick space on the end side, as well as on the kitchen side, so a person can work at the end. Depending on the use of the peninsula, it might be necessary to have kick space on both sides of all the base cabinets.

The wall cabinet run should be shorter than the base cabinet run. This prevents head bumping and also contributes to a more open appearance to the kitchen.

When ordering wall cabinets for use in a peninsula, the buyer should specify that they are for peninsular use. The cabinet manufacturer will add extra reinforcing at the top of these cabinets—maybe. If they do not come with reinforcing, it will have to be provided by the installer.

The countertop at the end of the peninsula should have radiused corners for safety. Square corners will lead to bruised hands and hips forever.

All of these considerations apply also to islands.

If a cooktop is used in either a peninsula or an island it probably will need some sort of backsplash or other barrier to protect others from grease spatters, hot handles, and the like.

27 SUCCESSFUL KITCHEN FLOORPLANS

The Kitchen Design Studio of General Electric Company and Hotpoint has designed at least 25,000 kitchens for builders and architects in the last 15 years, kitchens which have been installed in hundreds of thousands of new homes.

Specifically for this book, Department Manager William J. Ketcham selected 27 floorplans that represent good design principles well worth emulating.

All are drawn to 1/4" scale.

In some cases extended areas of the house are included because of the way the kitchen inter-relates. In one case, two different floorplans are included for the same kitchen, one in Corridor and the other in L-shape configuration, showing how variations are possible for cause. In this case, the Corridor kept all cross-traffic out of the kitchen, but the L permitted access to the bathroom from the kitchen.

In many cases the laundry area is included in the floorplan. The laundry is never recommended *in* the kitchen, but it often is wanted near the kitchen, with access.

Floorplan abbreviations: REFR—refrigerator; DW—dishwasher; RA—range; COMP—trash compactor; W—clothes washer and D—dryer.

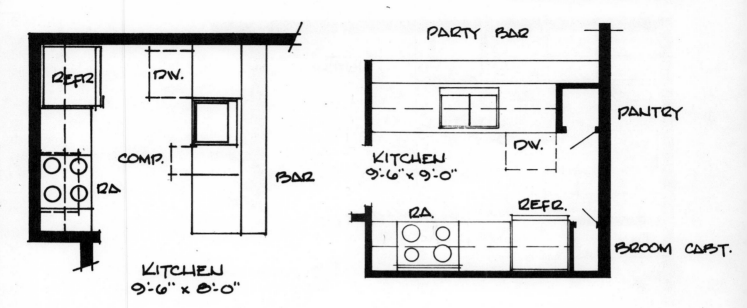

REFR

DW.

COMP.

RA

BAR

KITCHEN
9'-6" x 8'-0"

1.

PARTY BAR

DW.

KITCHEN
9'-6" x 9'-0"

RA.

REFR.

PANTRY

BROOM CABT.

2.

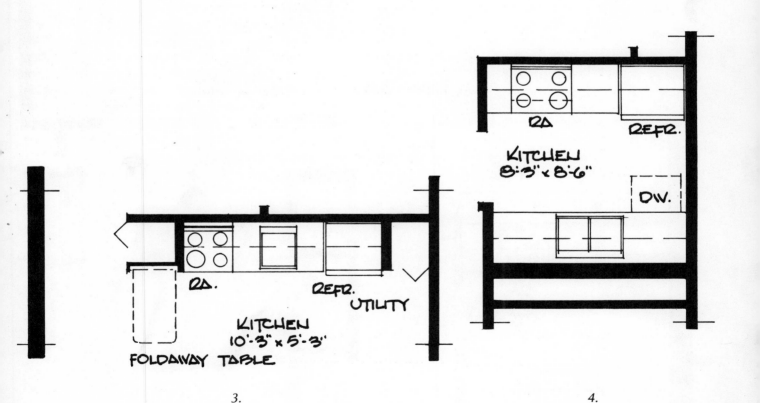

RA.

REFR.

UTILITY

KITCHEN
10'-3" x 5'-3"

FOLDAWAY TABLE

3.

RA

REFR.

KITCHEN
8'-3" x 8'-6"

DW.

4.

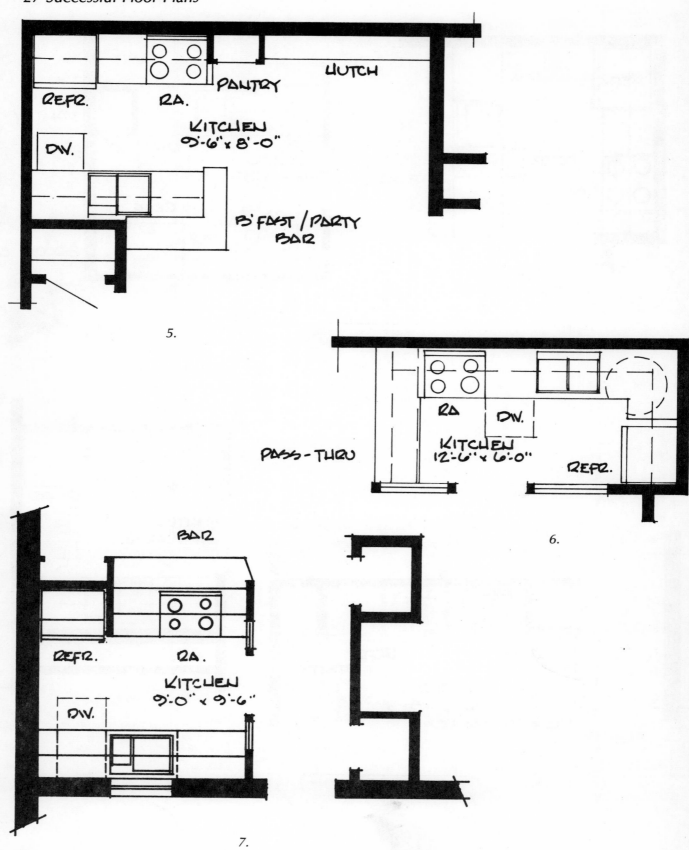

REFR.

RA.

PANTRY

HUTCH

KITCHEN
9'-6" x 8'-0"

DW.

B'FAST / PARTY
BAR

5.

PASS-THRU

RA

DW.

KITCHEN
12'-6" x 6'-0"

REFR.

6.

BAR

REFR.

RA.

KITCHEN
9'-0" x 9'-6"

DW.

7.

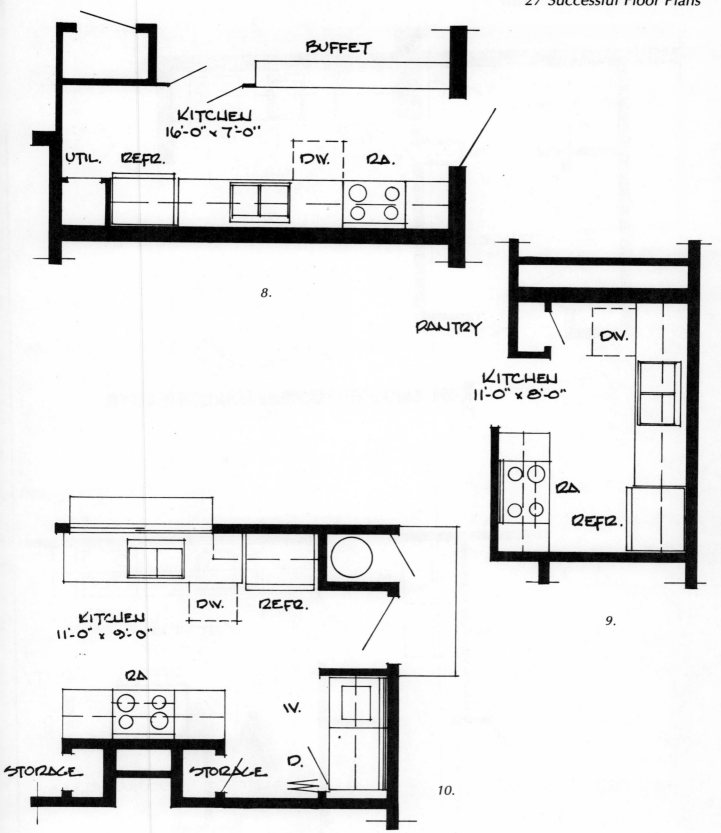

BUFFET

KITCHEN
16'-0" x 7'-0"

UTIL. REFR. DW. RA.

8.

PANTRY

KITCHEN
11'-0" x 8'-0"

DW.

RA.

REFR.

9.

KITCHEN
11'-0" x 9'-0"

DW. REFR.

RA.

IV.

D.

STORAGE STORAGE

10.

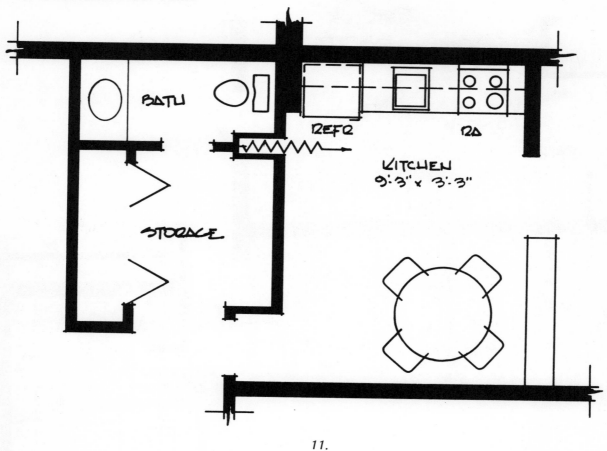

BATH

REFR

RA

KITCHEN
9'-3" x 3'-3"

STORAGE

11.

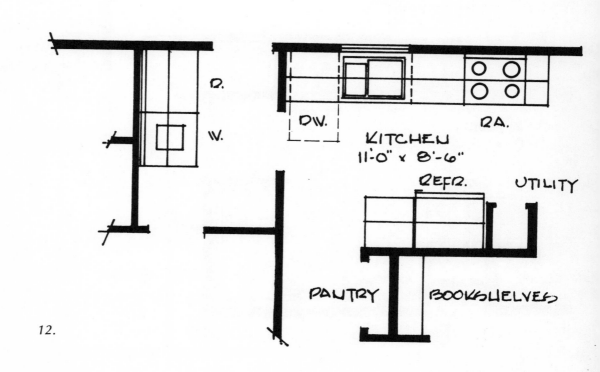

D.

W.

DW.

RA.

KITCHEN
11'-0" x 8'-6"

REFR.

UTILITY

PANTRY

BOOKSHELVES

12.

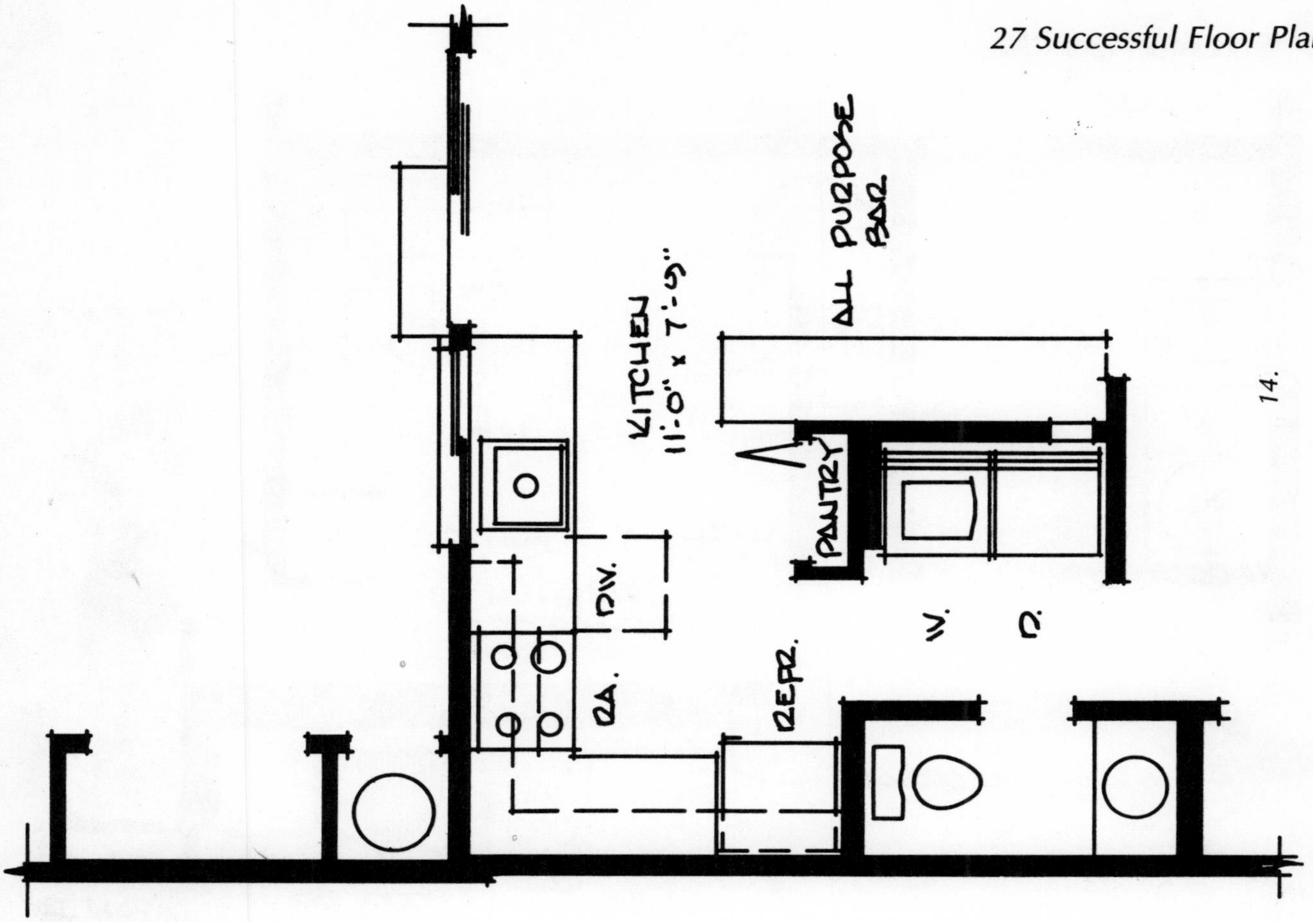

KITCHEN 11'-0" x 7'-9"

ALL PURPOSE ROOM

PANTRY

DW.

RA.

REFR.

D.

W.

14.

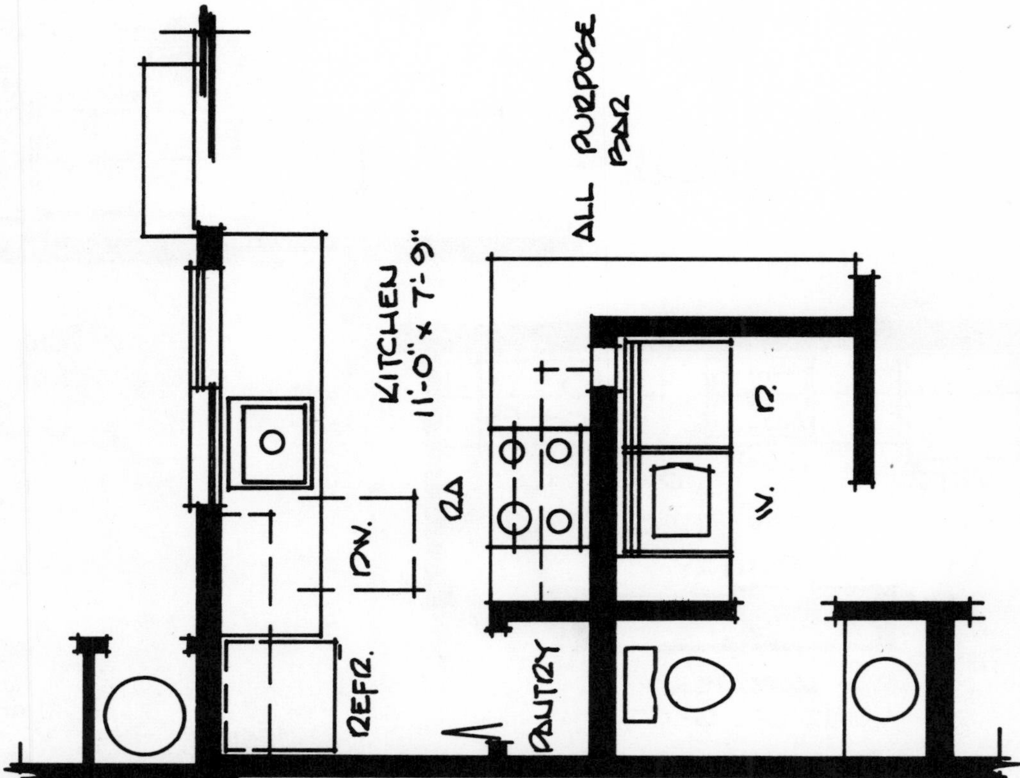

KITCHEN 11'-0" x 7'-9"

ALL PURPOSE ROOM

RA

DW.

REFR.

PANTRY

D.

W.

13.

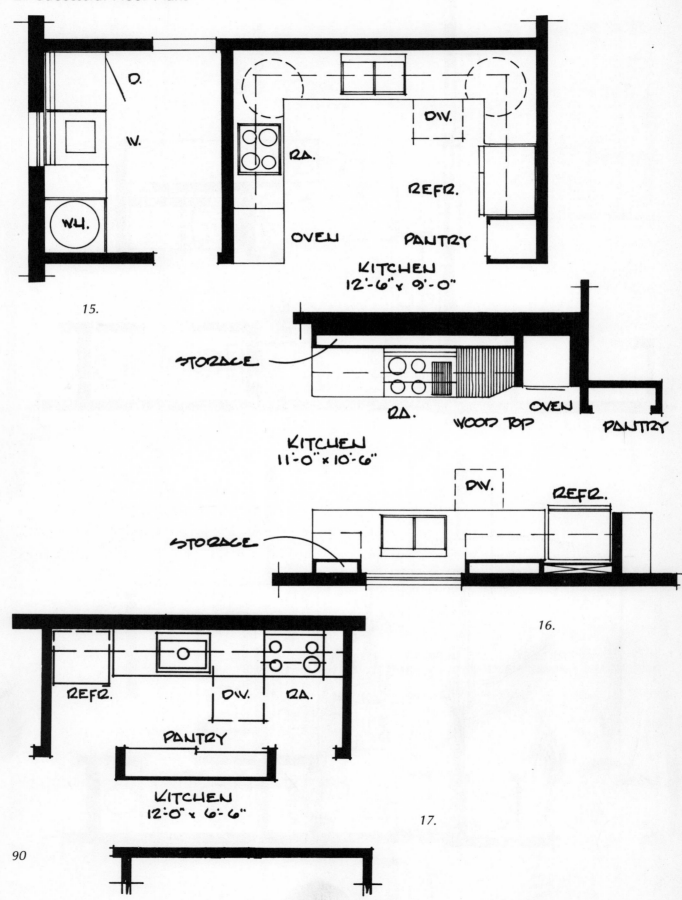

D.

W.

WH.

DW.

RA.

REFR.

OVEN

PANTRY

KITCHEN
12'-6" x 9'-0"

15.

STORAGE

RA.

WOOD TOP

OVEN

PANTRY

KITCHEN
11'-0" x 10'-6"

DW.

REFR.

STORAGE

16.

REFR.

DW.

RA.

PANTRY

KITCHEN
12'-0" x 6'-6"

17.

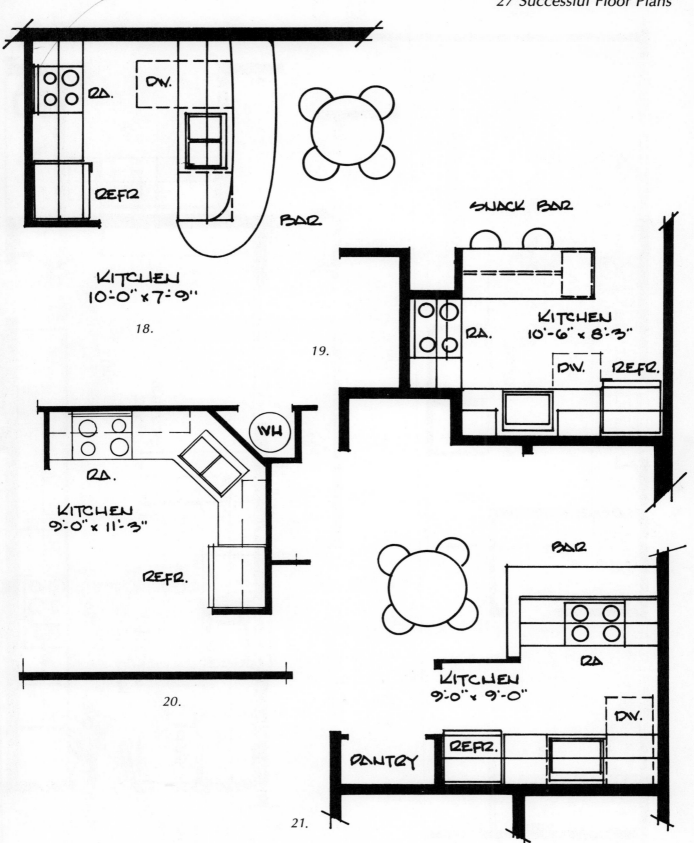

KITCHEN
10'-0" x 7'-9"

18.

19.

SNACK BAR

KITCHEN
10'-6" x 8'-3"

KITCHEN
9'-0" x 11'-3"

20.

BAR

KITCHEN
9'-0" x 9'-0"

PANTRY

21.

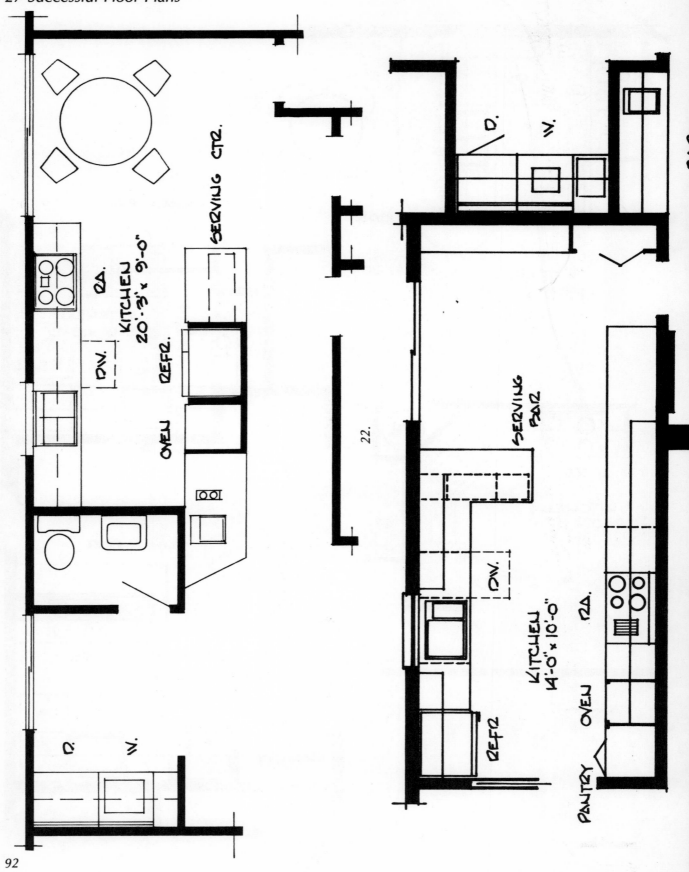

KITCHEN
20'-3" x 9'-0"

RA.

DW.

REFR.

OVEN

SERVING CTR.

D.

W.

22.

SERVING BAR

DW.

KITCHEN
14'-0" x 10'-0"

D.

W.

REFR.

PANTRY

OVEN

RA.

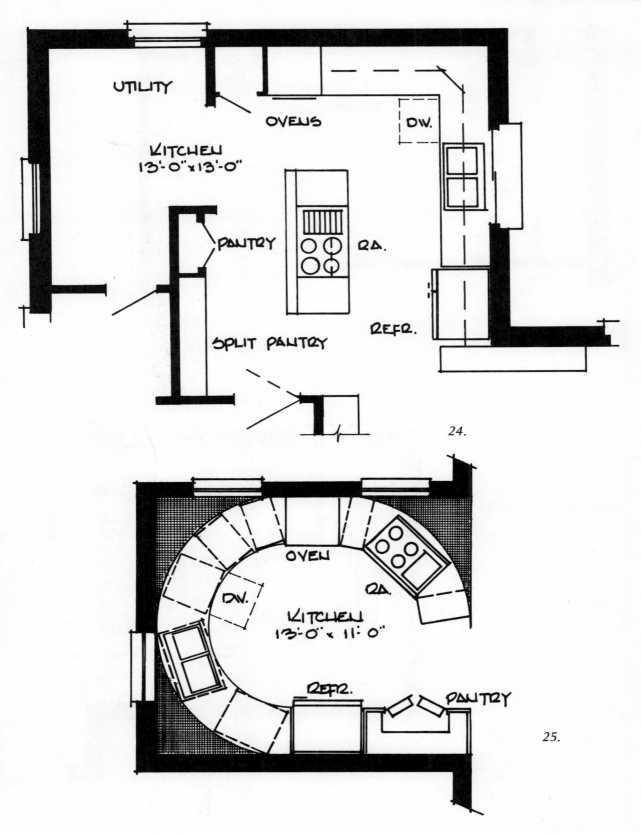

UTILITY

OVENS

KITCHEN
13'-0" x 13'-0"

DW.

PANTRY

RA.

REFR.

SPLIT PANTRY

24.

OVEN

DW.

RA.

KITCHEN
13'-0" x 11'-0"

REFR.

PANTRY

25.

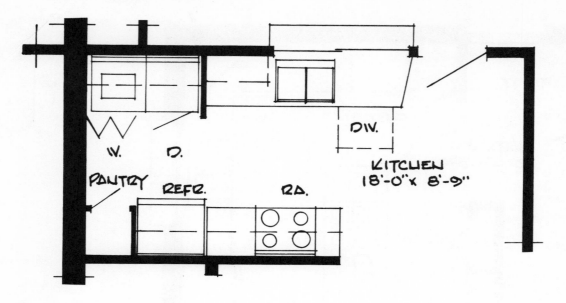

W.   D.

PANTRY   REFR.   RA.

DW.

KITCHEN
18'-0" x 8'-9"

26.

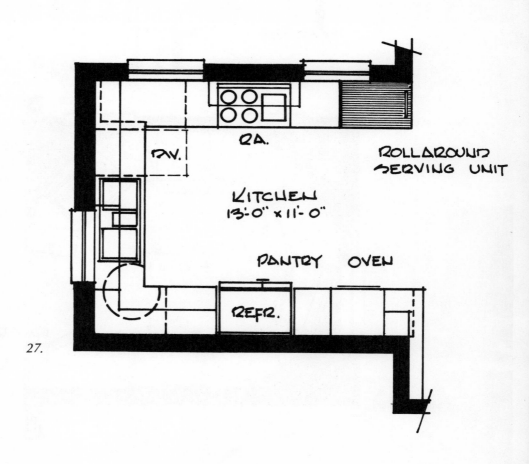

DW.

RA.

ROLLAROUND
SERVING UNIT

KITCHEN
13'-0" x 11'-0"

PANTRY   OVEN

REFR.

27.

Quaker Maid's Clarion cabinets are used in this spacious kitchen which includes even a fireplace. Notice the large wood-framed ventilating hood which serves cooking island that has both a cooktop and a barbecue grill.

A built-in Sub-Zero refrigerator was used in this kitchen, and decorator panels matching the cabinets were used on both refrigerator and KitchenAid dishwasher to integrate the design.

Textures and contrasts are the story in this kitchen, small but complete. Cabinets are wood, painted white to contrast with black decorative hinges and pulls.

Kemper's Manor Oak cabinets form a cooking island in this kitchen, giving a work triangle not interrupted by passing traffic.

U-shaped kitchen designed by Howard Sersen of Reynolds Enterprises, River Grove, Ill., has wood beams to frame the chandelier. Countertop is angled at corner to avoid constricting the entrance, and corners are radiused to prevent hip bruises.

House & Garden magazine's 1972 "Super Family Room Kitchen" has a complete wall of equipment that disappears behind folding doors. The wall includes double wall oven, dishwasher, sink and refrigerator (all showing) plus incinerator, heater and laundry.

Yes, there are round kitchens. This unusual one has solid maple countertops and a space-saving drop-in range. Open shelving demands extra neatness from the housewife. Floor covering here is Armstrong's Carriage Park cushioned vinyl.

This is a real wrap-around kitchen, but the island cooking center keeps the work triangle tight and the eating counter in the foreground is great for entertaining. Cabinets are Kemper's Cortina, an oak line.

Super kitchen by Modern Kitchens of Syracuse (N.Y.)
has built-in refrigerator at far end, double wall ovens
in brick wall, barbecue under brick arch.

Bisulk Kitchens, Garden City, N.Y. used
Dacor artificial brick for this cooking wall
with Waste-King double wall oven.
Designer put the wood beam across
cooking alcove to hide vent equipment and
lighting, made the crisscrosses on base
cabinets himself to add to ambience.

Spacious cooking island by Kennedy Kitchens, Horseheads, N.Y., has a properly-raised section behind Thermador cooktop to form protective backsplash. It also has food warming drawer at bottom left. But the brightest idea shows in background—

—This opening in the cabinet wall, beside the built-in refrigerator, has AM-FM radio-intercom at top, infra-red warming light recessed along with a matching white flood (because you can't really see by infra-red) and even a convenience outlet at back.

Another bright idea in the same Kennedy kitchen is this lowered work surface with maple block top. Kennedy studied some kitchen research at Cornell University, found that most work surfaces were too high for most women. That's a Trade-Wind built-in can opener in wall.

Another Betterhouse kitchen has candlelight fixtures mounted on two blank wall cabinets flanking sink, recessed shelf over sink, spice box recessed into wall over Corning cooktop.

Swiss Chalet kitchen by Betterhouse, Wyoming, Pa., combines with family entertainment center at other side of same large room. Woodlike beams are Williams polyurethane. Curved doors in mixing center island are exclusive with MarVell.

Wood-beamed ceiling complements the Quaker Maid cabinets in this kitchen by Kitchens, Inc., Narrowsburg, N.Y. Plastic-laminate-covered window box pushes sink out from wall, so countertop was made to protrude to compensate.

Totally different Mediterranean effect by Ray Swearingen Co. of Chevy Chase, Md., uses Keystone white glacial ash cabinets with colorful bullfighters on front of island.

Betterhouse specializes in innovative cover-ups for peninsulas that face other rooms. Here carpet is run up the front of the peninsula and glued.

Kitchens by Krengel, St. Paul, Minn., was designed first and then the home was built to fit it. Kitchen sink is at far wall. Center island has two Corning cooktops. Near island has a bar sink plus eating bar. Circular soffit defines kitchen area. Cabinets are solid cherry by Keystone.

7

Lighting in the Kitchen

As a last resort, one can go to the statistics of the National Safety Council to underscore the need for good lighting in the kitchen. According to the NSC the kitchen is the most dangerous room in the home, accounting for 1,150,000 accidents per year, 26 percent of all falls and burns in the home, and 12 percent of all home fatalities.

All of these accidents are chiefly the results of poor illumination, according to the council.

But who needs last resorts? Lighting has a lot more going for it than the threat of accident.

It's useful, enabling us to see quickly and easily.

It can contribute to the beauty and individuality of the kitchen and the entire home. It even can be the salient feature of overall decor, if one wants to use it that creatively.

Unfortunately, the single ceiling fixture in the kitchen still is too much with us. It dates back to past decades when putting more light in the kitchen could be accomplished only by putting in a bigger bulb and hoping the fuse wouldn't blow.

It still probably is the most common way to light a kitchen, although modified now by a somewhat more modern fixture with three or four smaller bulbs and a much more efficient diffusing shield, or shade.

This is adequate, if bright enough, but adequacy does not add the charm that sells homes or makes an efficient kitchen.

This chapter will tell specifically how much light to use and where to put it, but first, the elementary facts of light.

In the planning stage and in choosing products, there are three basic terms that need definition.

The *candela* is the unit of luminous intensity of a light source in a specific direction. While its precise definition may be more than anyone really wants to know, for those interested it is 1/60 of the intensity of a square centimeter of a black body radiator operated at the freezing point of platinum, which is 2047 degrees Kelvin.

A *lumen* is the unit for measuring the light-producing power of a light source, and lamps are usually rated by their total lumen output. A lumen is the rate at which light falls on a one-square-foot area surface from a source which has an intensity of one candela. The number of lumens per watt indicates the efficiency of the light source.

A *footlambert* is a unit for measuring the brightness of light emitted or reflected from a surface directly into the eye at the rate of one lumen per square foot of area as viewed from any direction.

Light in the kitchen, as in other rooms of the house, usually is expressed in terms of watts. This is sufficient only when related to distance from light source to use area, transmittance through whatever shades are used, reflectance from all kitchen surfaces (which can make a tremendous difference in lighting efficiency) and absorptance, which is the amount of light lost by being absorbed by dark surfaces.

All of those factors can be calculated but, practically speaking, common sense can be relied on to make sure there is enough light—if it is educated common sense. This is an area where the advice of an architect or expert who understands technicalities of absorption or reflection may help greatly.

The ultimate proof of lighting efficiency is measurement of the lumens in the various areas of the kitchen. They can be measured by using a General Electric light meter available from any photographic store or from the GE Large Lamp Department, Nela Park, Cleveland. (There are many brands of light meters, but many of them do not read in lumens, hence cannot be used for this purpose.)

Nela Park, incidentally, is a virtual university of lighting knowledge and techniques. Short courses are available there and many booklets are available, notably *Residential Structural Lighting* and *Light Measurement and Control.*

There are three sources of light to be considered in kitchen design:

1. *Natural daylight,* available through
   a. Windows, bright and cheerful in the morning with east exposure, miserable in late afternoon if exposure is west. No factor at night.
   b. Skylights, available in transparent or translucent plastics and a great sales point.
2. *Incandescent light,* from bulbs available in various shapes and sizes ranging from small night lights up to 300 watts. This light is produced by heating any material, usually metal, to a temperature at which it glows. Usually bulbs have a tungsten filament in a vacuum or mixture of argon and nitrogen.
   a. Bulbs can be clear or frosted, or colored to give a warmer light.
   b. Special types have reflector surfaces so they can be directed upward for indirect lighting, or downward for spot or floodlighting, broad or narrow beam.
3. *Fluorescent light,* glass tubes coated on the inside with fluorescent powder, filled with vaporized mercury and argon and sealed with two cathodes. Electric current activates the gas which produces invisible ultraviolet rays which causes the powder coating to fluoresce, producing visible light.
   a. All bulbs are tubular, but they might be straight or circular.
   b. Straight tubes vary generally from 9 to 60 inches and 6 to 100 watts. Length of the tube is a factor in the wattage.
   c. Color choices are all shades of white including Daylight, which emphasizes blues and greens; White, emphasizing yellows and yellow greens; Standard Cool White and Standard Warm White, lacking in reds; Deluxe Cool White and Deluxe Warm White, with some reds; Soft White, good for pinks and tans.

d. Deluxe Warm White is generally most satisfactory.

Incandescent and fluorescent bulbs both have their advantages, and that means it is a good idea to use a mixture of both in the kitchen.

Advantages of incandescence are:

1) Fixtures and bulbs are less costly.
2) Light is warmer and generally more acceptable because we are accustomed to it.
3) Textures and forms usually are more attractive because the light comes from a relatively small source.
4) The light is instant-on.
5) There is no flicker or hum, as is often the case with fluorescence, and less chance of interference with radio or television.

Advantages for fluorescent tubes include:

1) Much more efficient light production, about 250 percent more than incandescence for the current used.
2) Bulbs last about seven times longer than incandescent bulbs.
3) Large light source produces much less glare and spreads the light more.
4) Almost no heat is produced, whereas incandescent bulbs are a definite heat factor.

In planning for lighting, bulbs and tubes can be mixed. For example, the heat and glare factors are insignificant if an incandescent ceiling fixture is used for general lighting, and here the instant-on factor would be valuable. So the planner might want this pleasant general illumination.

But the planner also must have sufficient glareless light where it is needed for close work, and good illumination at danger points, and there must be an esthetic consideration—the lighting should add to the beauty of the kitchen.

If the cabinets in the kitchen are dark the quantity of light must be increased, since dark surfaces absorb a lot of light. Dark flooring also calls for more light.

A dim light level tends to be relaxing and restful.

A bright light level tends to be stimulating and makes people feel more energetic.

Lights at eye-level are not desirable, usually, and must be well shielded so they do not shine directly

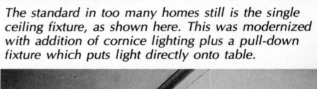

Well-lighted kitchen has general lighting, as provided by this cornice installation that shines light both above and below, plus task lighting as is gained here from fixtures below wall cabinets.

The standard in too many homes still is the single ceiling fixture, as shown here. This was modernized with addition of cornice lighting plus a pull-down fixture which puts light directly onto table.

Here a full luminous ceiling is the best of all, affording generous general light, supplemented by task lighting under wall cabinets. (AIKD photo).

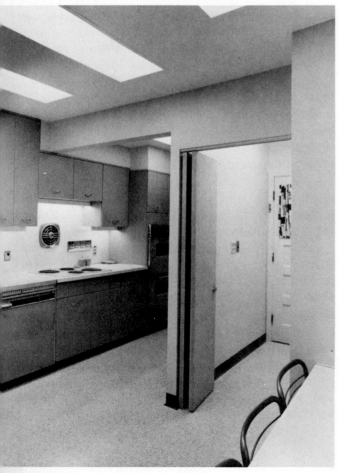

Another well-lighted kitchen has luminous ceiling panels for general light, fixtures under all wall cabinets.

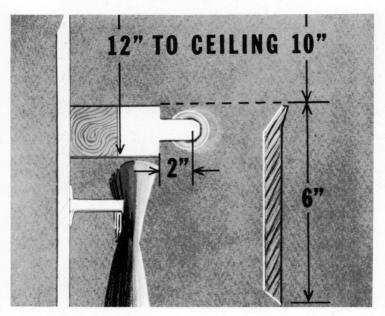

Structural lighting offers good solutions for the kitchen as well as for other rooms in the house. This drawing shows recommendations for a valance lighting installation. Faceboards should be not less than 6", not more than 10". Inside should always be painted flat white.

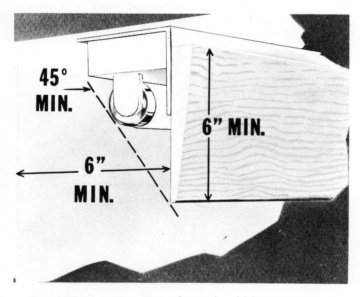

In cornice construction, there should be 2" to 3" between center of fluorescent tube and surface to be lighted. Faceboard should be painted flat white on inside, and channel should be as close to faceboard as possible.

into the eyes. Lights at levels high in the room tend to seem formal, and lights below eye-level seem friendly and attractive. But here again, they should not shine directly into the eyes.

Warm light is flattering to people and good for warm color schemes in the kitchen, but it deadens the blue end of the spectrum. Cool light is unflattering to people, but it adds to a sense of spaciousness. A favorable combination of these qualities would use warm light for general illumination and cool light for more specific lighting, but probably the best over-all solution, in the absence of an expert to develop special lighting effects, is to combine warm incandescence with warm fluorescent tubes.

All lighting experts and all kitchen experts and all home economists (and all lighting salesmen) will recommend two types of lighting in any kitchen:

1) General illumination, such as might be provided by the single ceiling fixture, an illuminated ceiling or perimeter soffit fixtures.
2) Task lighting, which puts light from separate sources directly onto specific work areas.

For general lighting, the American Home Lighting Institute recommends one fixture for every 50 square feet of area.

Each fixture should contain from 175 to 200 watts if incandescent, with a minimum 14-inch diameter for the fixture, or 60 to 80 watts if fluorescent; or, if the floor area of the kitchen is no more than 50 square feet, one suspended luminous-ceiling fixture measuring 24 square feet and with at least 360 watts incandescence.

For a fluorescent luminous ceiling in this application, the minimum depth from louvers to tube centers is 8 inches. A 40-watt tube is needed for every 12 square feet of room area. With incandescent bulbs, a 60-watt bulb is needed for every square feet of panel.

This applies, of course, for a normal, 8-foot ceiling. Light loses its effectiveness inversely with the square of the distance, and a 10-foot ceiling would call for more light. The visual criterion is that the general illumination should give adequate vision into drawers and cabinets, and there should be no difficulty reading labels.

Task lighting is needed in all food preparation areas along the countertop, over the range, over the sink, and at any other place where specific tasks are performed.

For countertop work surfaces, a fluorescent tube mounted at the bottom front of the overhanging wall cabinet will be about 15 inches above the counter, normally, and this calls for one 20-watt tube for every three feet of counter.

To break this down to a practical situation, this means a 20-watt tube for from 24 to 36 inches of counter; a 30-watt tube for from 36 to 48 inches of counter, and a 40-watt tube for from 48 to 60 inches of counter.

This wattage is good for up to 22 inches above the counter, a height that is unfortunately high for wall cabinets, but it is not uncommon in cost-cutting kitchens.

A 2-socket incandescent bracket with 60 watts in each socket is the equivalent for each three feet of counter, but the fluorescent tube adapts so easily to this application that there is little reason to make the job harder with incandescence. Overhang of the wall cabinet's face frame often provides all the shielding necessary for a fluorescent tube.

If there is no wall cabinet, the tube will have to be shielded fully so it does not shine in the eyes. In this case it will be wall-mounted with the tube toward the front. When a standard channel fixture is mounted at the bottom front of a wall cabinet, the tube goes toward the rear. In this case shielding will not be needed even if there is no face frame overhang, as long as the wall cabinet is at standard height—51 inches from the floor.

Task lighting over the sink may come from the ceiling or the soffit, or it may be wall-mounted.

From ceiling or soffit, a situation where normally there is a window flanked by cabinets, there can be:

1) One recessed fixture with three 75-watt incandescent bulbs in a box at least 24 inches long, or two 40-watt or three 30-watt fluorescent tubes, or

2) Two recessed fixtures with inner reflectors with a 100-watt incandescent bulb in each, centered 18 inches apart, or

3) Two, or preferably three, bullets which might be recessed, pendant or surface-mounted, each with a 75-watt flood bulb.

All of these might or might not be shielded by a face frame connecting the flanking wall cabinets.

The same requirements apply to a cooktop or range in this location. But a range is usually mounted under

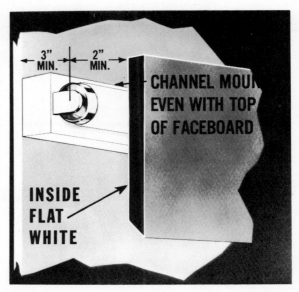

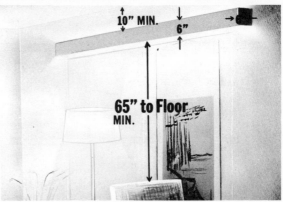

Wall brackets are most useful in structural lighting. The high wall bracket is really a valance without a window. Bracket must be high so light will spread over ceiling.

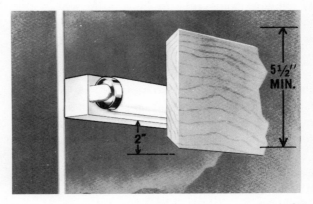

Low wall brackets are good for local or task lighting. Lamp should not be lower than 2" above bottom of shield. These are not used at more than 65" from floor.

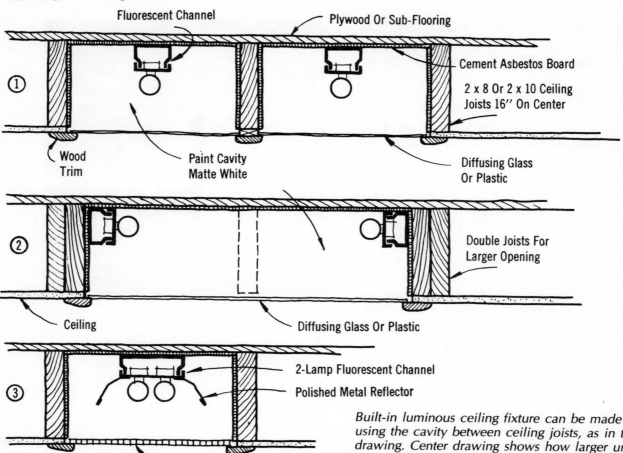

Built-in luminous ceiling fixture can be made by using the cavity between ceiling joists, as in top drawing. Center drawing shows how larger units may be framed-in to desired shape by cutting out center joist and using double framing. Lamp arrangement shown is for decorative, non-uniform effect. Where more light is desired, two lamps with reflectors can be used, using louver as bottom shield instead of diffusing plastic.

a plain wall, with a hood 24 inches above and a cabinet above the hood. The hood should have one or two incandescent sockets or tubes.

If there is no hood there should be a wall bracket mounted from 14 to 22 inches above the range (or sink) allowing some upward light. Minimum is one 30-watt fluorescent tube or multiple-socket incandescent in a box at least 18 inches long with 60 or 75 watts in each socket.

A dining area in the kitchen area (not a brunch counter) requires separate illumination, even though it will benefit from the lighting in the kitchen.

Incandescence is favored here. It makes food look better and it is more flattering to the people and the colors of dishes and clothing.

It requires at least 150 watts in a fixture that directs light both upward and downward. A close-to-ceiling pendant fixture, or other suspended fixture, should be at least 17 inches in diameter, single or multiple sockets.

If fluorescence is used, a wall bracket would require one 36-inch 30-watt Deluxe Warm White tube, and light should be directed both upward and downward.

A brunch area in the kitchen that uses a countertop can use the same task lighting that has been installed for food preparation, but if any light is added, it should be consistent in design with the kitchen lighting. A higher intensity is called for here, as compared with the dining area, because brighter light makes people feel more energetic, as they would want to feel at breakfast or lunch time.

In this chapter there have been various references to the effect of light on color. It should be remembered that light and color are so inter-related that there really is no such thing as a light that shows color "as it really is." Color is a function of light. For more on this, see Chapter 8, which discusses the use of color in the kitchen.

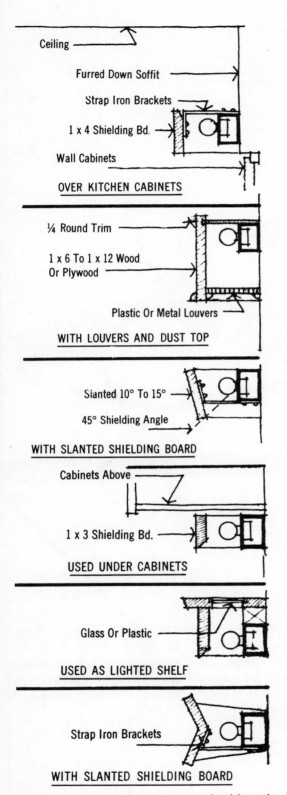

OVER KITCHEN CABINETS

- Ceiling
- Furred Down Soffit
- Strap Iron Brackets
- 1 x 4 Shielding Bd.
- Wall Cabinets

WITH LOUVERS AND DUST TOP

- ¼ Round Trim
- 1 x 6 To 1 x 12 Wood Or Plywood
- Plastic Or Metal Louvers

WITH SLANTED SHIELDING BOARD

- Slanted 10° To 15°
- 45° Shielding Angle

USED UNDER CABINETS

- Cabinets Above
- 1 x 3 Shielding Bd.

USED AS LIGHTED SHELF

- Glass Or Plastic

WITH SLANTED SHIELDING BOARD

- Strap Iron Brackets

Here are some of the options in building the light on the job in the kitchen, for over the cabinets, shelving or under the wall cabinets.

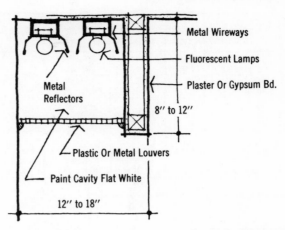

- Metal Wireways
- Fluorescent Lamps
- Plaster Or Gypsum Bd.
- Metal Reflectors
- 8″ to 12″
- Plastic Or Metal Louvers
- Paint Cavity Flat White
- 12″ to 18″

When soffit over work area must provide a high level of light directly below, polished reflectors can double light output when used with open louvers. Only two rows of lamps are needed when polished metal reflectors are used.

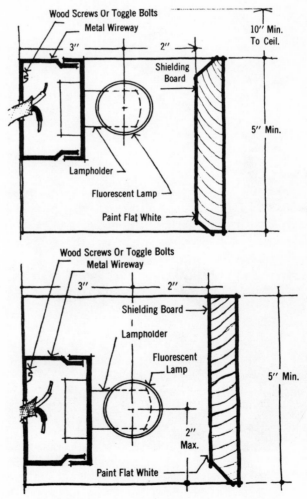

- Wood Screws Or Toggle Bolts
- Metal Wireway
- 3″
- 2″
- 10″ Min. To Ceil.
- Shielding Board
- 5″ Min.
- Lampholder
- Fluorescent Lamp
- Paint Flat White

- Wood Screws Or Toggle Bolts
- Metal Wireway
- 3″
- 2″
- Shielding Board
- Lampholder
- Fluorescent Lamp
- 5″ Min.
- 2″ Max.
- Paint Flat White

Detail of high and low type wall brackets.

Soffit Data; Lighting Photos

Location	Use	Cavity Dimensions				Deluxe Warm White Lamps	Parabolic Aluminum Reflectors	Material for Bottom Closure
		Depth	Width	Length	Finish			
Kitchen	Over sink or work center	8 to 12 in.	12 in.	38 in. min	Flat white	Two rows to fill length. Two 30-watt minimum.	Yes	Louvers
Bath or Dressing Room	Over large mirror	8 in.	14 to 18 in.	Length of mirror	Flat white	Two rows to fill length. Two 40-watt minimum.	No	White diffusing glass or plastic
		8 in.	18 to 24 in.	Length of mirror	Flat white	Three rows to fill length. Three 40-w. minimum.	No	White diffusing glass or plastic
								Lightly etched material acceptable
Living Area	Over piano, desk, sofa, or other seeing area	10 in.	Fit space Available 12 in. min	Fit Space Available 50 in. min	Flat white except matte black painted back wall surface	Two rows to fill length. Two 40-watt minimum.	Yes	Lightly figured or etched glass or plastic

Soffit construction data, as recommended by Nela Park.

Lighting fixture manufacturers make "false" luminous panel lights also, as well as fixtures that recess. Recessed squares are by Progress Lighting. Progress, Lightolier and NuTone are among those who make the types that attach below the ceiling.

Everything is plastic laminated in this, by Kennedy Kitchens, Horseheads, N.Y., including walls and ceiling. Horizontal panel over cooktop, just left of built-in oven, actually hides a fluorescent tube (and vent fan) which gives interesting wash of light above and below.

Those are windows under the wall cabinets in this kitchen by Charlotte Clark Kitchens, Detroit, a very unusual design feature. Fluorescent lighting is hidden above, where slope of ceiling meets tops of wall cabinets. Cabinets are plastic laminated, by National Industries.

Fluorescent luminous ceiling panels located over work areas are supplemented by lights under the hood and a dramatic pendant fixture.
(Hedrich-Blessing photo)

Well-designed small kitchen lighted by carefully located ceiling fixtures and a light under the hood.
(Suter, Hedrich-Blessing photo)

"Bullet" fixtures light work areas, supplemented by borrowed light from the dining area. (Bill Engdahl, Hedrich-Blessing photo)

Antique lanterns provide accent lighting in colonial kitchen. (Hedrich-Blessing photo)

8

Color in the Kitchen

Color is possibly the most-used and least-understood phenomenon of both our physical and psychological worlds. It can be defined in terms of pigments and dyes, but the definition will fall short because it ignores both sensation and light. Some theorists insist it really is a sensation relating very personally to the viewer.

Anyone who buys a bright red car, parks it in daytime and then tries to find it later under a mercury street light will attest to the fact that color is very much a function of light source.

The consumer may become confused by the vagaries of light and color. A homeowner may visit a kitchen showroom and select cabinets for their warm, rich, reddish woodtones. When they are installed in his home, however, they may appear flat and gray. But he got the right cabinets. The difference in this case was that the showroom was lit by incandescent bulbs and his kitchen was lit by fluorescence.

Light has its peculiarities. We call it white light, but when it is directed through an optical prism we find it contains all colors, splitting up into a spectrum ranging from infrared to ultraviolet. This is white light, and with all those colors in it, light itself is invisible. Yet without it, everything else is invisible.

There are three primary colors, but they are different for light and for pigments.

The primary colors of light are red, green, and blue. They are called additive primaries because they can be added to produce the secondary colors, magenta (red plus blue), cyan (green plus blue), and yellow (red plus green). A secondary color of light, mixed with its opposite primary, will give white light.

Primary colors in pigments are magenta, cyan, and yellow. These are subtractive primaries because in pigments a primary color is defined as one that

subtracts, or absorbs a primary color of light and reflects the other two.

To get familiar with all the terms:

1) Hue is the name of the color.
2) The lightness or darkness of a color is its value.
   a. Adding black to a color gives a shade.
   b. Adding white to a color gives a tint.
   c. Adding gray gives a tone.
3) A color's purity or strength is called its intensity.

Complementary hues are those directly *opposite* each other on the color wheel. Analogous hues are those *next* to each other. *(for a typical color wheel, see page 24.)*

To mix complementary hues is to neutralize. If you physically mixed the pigments you would end up with a neutral gray, but putting them next to each other adds contrast—extreme contrast.

Extreme contrast is great, if not overdone. If the entire color scheme of a room is based solely on contrast, the result is disastrous.

In a kitchen the elements to consider for color are the cabinets, the appliances, the countertops, the ceiling, the walls, and the floor. Beyond that, accessories can be color highlights.

The procedure is:

1) Establish the dominating color.
2) Decide where it will go.
3) Using the color wheel, establish the complementary colors.
4) Decide where they will go.

For the dominating color—and by dominating, here, we mean the one that will be most generally used in the kitchen—you might decide on the popular avocado, which is a green. The color wheel shows red directly across, so some red will have to be used in the kitchen. There might be avocado cabinets, and the green could be picked up in a lighter tint in the soffit and on the ceiling. There could be a dramatic red countertop, or even red appliances, or the red might be only a curtain at the window. Red would have to be there somewhere.

You might choose a blend of greens and yellows for cabinets, countertop, appliances, walls, and ceiling. Directly across the wheel from green and yellow is red-purple, and even a simple dish display on a wall in this tertiary color would suffice. But it must be there, however small.

Here are some other points to remember:

1) You cannot get appliance and cabinet colors to match exactly. So use complementary colors, or contrasting shades of the same color.
2) Usually, the fewer colors used the better, and keep window and door trim the same color as the walls.
3) Color intensifies in a north room or in a small room, so use tints except for accents.
4) North light is cold. If the room has a north window it is best to use colors from the warm side of the wheel with the cold colors for accents.
5) A strong color on the ceiling tends to make the ceiling "come down" oppressively. Use very light colors on the ceiling or keep it neutral gray or white.
6) It usually is better to keep darker colors lower in the kitchen than the countertop.

7) Remember the lighting. Incandescence can brighten warm colors, such as yellow. Blue shaded toward green can appear green when the lights are on.
8) An *expensive* dish or drape can furnish a ready-made color scheme. Such expensive items are not color-keyed by cheap labor. They are designed by the best color brains in the business.
9) Warm hues are conspicuous, cheerful, stimulating. They appear to come toward you, to pull things together, to make objects look larger.
10) Cool hues are more restful, separate things, and make objects look smaller. They can be cold and depressing.
(There is a physiological explanation for some of that. Red rays register behind the eye's retina, and the eye pulls them forward simply by pulling them into focus. Cool rays register in front of the retina and are pushed back in focusing.)
11) While warm hues *increase* the apparent size of things within a room, when these hues are used as wall colors they *decrease* the apparent size of the room. The same is true of high intensities. Sharp contrast brings objects forward.
12) Be sure colors are selected under the same lighting conditions as will exist in the kitchen. All colors, even white and black, will look different under fluorescence and under incandescence.
13) If there is a lot of natural light in the kitchen, dark colors can be used more effectively. If the kitchen must depend on artificial light, lighter colors are usually more satisfactory.

9

Floors, Walls and Ceilings

Floorcovering is one of the most important parts of the kitchen because it is one of the most readily noticeable design elements. It affects color scheme. It affects lighting. It can help make the room seem larger or smaller, warmer or colder.

The first choice that must be made is between carpeting and resilient floorcovering.

The resilients dominate by far. As a category there are no bad ones, although some are better than others. They range from cheap to expensive, and the really good ones incorporate softness without sacrificing durability.

Carpeting is used more in remodeled kitchens, although still far outdistanced by resilients. It puts a real luxury look and feel into a kitchen and, despite its critics, it is very practical. It does, however, arouse considerable sales resistance among people who have never tried it.

Here are the flooring choices, with their good and bad points.

1. *Asphalt Tile*—low in cost and resistant to alkali stains. This material is fairly easy to maintain and it can be installed directly over a concrete base below or above grade.

   However, it is only fair in resiliency and, being harder, is not as quiet as other materials. Lighter colors are much higher in price.

2. *Asbestos Vinyl Tile*—an improvement over asbestos tile, blending asbestos and vinyl for clearer, cleaner colors and more resiliency. It can be laid on, above or below grade. It is somewhat more expensive than asphalt tile. It is durable and stain resistant.

3. *Vinyl*—in tiles or sheets, plain or cushioned. In tiles, this is luxury material with excellent colors and patterns. In sheet form it is moderately priced. It is very durable and has superior resistance to stains and can be laid on, above or below grade. Tiles are fairly expensive, and any vinyl must be laid over very smooth base. It scratches fairly easily.

4. *Linoleum*—the well-known material is moderately priced, fairly durable, easy to maintain, but does not resist alkali stains very well. Very wide choices of colors and patterns, including sculptured and inlaid effects. It is somewhat porous and so needs good home maintenance to guard against ground-in dirt. Overall, a best buy, despite its deficiencies. Lay only on suspended floors.

5. *Others* include rubber tile, very quiet and very resilient with good resistance to grease and alkalis; vinyl cork tile, very expensive, but worth it; vinyl bonded ceramic tile, a new, very expensive product which overcomes many objections of ceramic tile because the little 1-inch tiles are embedded in vinyl, making it softer, quieter and more acceptable to the home buyer.

   For an ultra-luxury look, planners often use ceramic tile or experiment with genuine wood veneers embedded in clear plastic, offered only by Parkwood Laminates.

And then there is carpeting. The advent of man-made fibers such as nylon made it a suitable material for kitchen installation, and residential kitchen installations are known that date back to 1955.

Now there are several such chemical fibers, and

their comparative characteristics can be seen in the accompanying chart.

The important point to recognize is that kitchen carpet is not the same as indoor-outdoor carpet, although salesmen often tend to confuse this issue.

Indoor-outdoor carpet is a good, practical material for its application because water passes through it. It can be washed with a hose. This is great for a patio, but hardly practical in a kitchen.

Kitchen carpet, on the other hand, consists of a carpet surface separated from its sponge or foam backing by a water-proof bonding membrane. Water can not pass through it to the floor underlayment below. This means any spill—milk, eggs, or grease—can be washed up almost as easily as from resilient floorcovering. In the event of more serious damage, it can be patched easily. One brand, at least, even comes with a patching kit. It is a great kitchen flooring material.

Manufacturers recommend that a mastic be used to hold it tight to the floor. This author laid it loose, wall to wall and coved up into the kick-space of the cabinets, with 2-sided Scotch tape to hold it down at the two doorways, where it served for six years in a New York City apartment. It was then lifted and moved to a new suburban home, cut and patched to fit the new kitchen, with 2-sided tape used again to hold down all cut edges. The patchwork is absolutely undetectable, and it has served in the new home for four years and still looks like new. This is a good material.

Few things are more luxurious on a lazy Sunday morning.

Any flooring material must be chosen with design and color in mind. A small kitchen demands small patterns. A large kitchen can take bold motifs and large patterns. Stripes can add length or width to a room, adding the dimension in the direction of their axis.

Light colors are nearly always preferred for kitchen floors, unless a skilled decorator specifies otherwise for dramatic effect.

Walls

In the common concept, the walls of any kitchen are nearly covered with the cabinets and appliances,

so what is there to do with them except paint them?

That is one easy solution, but visit any good kitchen showroom for some surprising answers to what is possible and much more commendable.

A kitchen is a special place. Things happen there that don't happen anywhere else in the home, things such as food preparation and cooking and cleanup. There are differences in heat, humidity, and in the characteristics of the air. In addition, it is a separate enclave with its own design that usually is quite independent of the design characteristics of the rest of the house.

Here are some of the options.

1) Plastic brick or stone, a lifetime material that simulates the original very precisely, but is lightweight and easily cleaned. It can be used on a wall or a section of one wall, but if more than that is used it tends to dominate the room. It is good for the sides of islands or peninsulas.

2) Plastic laminate, the same as on the countertop, often is extended all the way from the countertop to the bottoms of the wall cabinets. This is an excellent treatment and is unbeatable for cleanability and neat appearance. It is not advisable behind a cooktop, however, because it can be darkened by the heat. It can be used on other walls and above the wall cabinets.

3) Panels of copper, stainless steel, porcelain enameled steel, or aluminum can be used behind a cooktop, in either sheet or tile form, for good protection and a very decorative effect.

4) Ordinary wall coverings can be decorative and effective, but they must not be of poor quality. A vinyl-coated wallpaper must be high quality to hold up under the necessary washing. A vinyl-coated fabric would be much better. When any of these are used, use large patterns only for large areas and small patterns for small areas. Light colors go best in small areas, and darker colors should be used only in large areas with good natural lighting.

5) Paint is the most common material for kitchen walls. A semigloss is best because enamels with their high gloss characteristics result in too much glare, and flat finishes are difficult to wash.

6) Vinyl-surfaced wall paneling can be very effective, especially in the light woodgrains. Darker woodgrains often are used to achieve separation of

In this kitchen (by Kitchen Concepts, Ft. Lauderdale, Fla.), desk area is covered by cabinetry, drape and shingled soffit above. Imitation brick is used for oven wall. Built-in Sub-Zero refrigerator occupies other wall.

Stucco and plaster also are favorites among kitchen specialists, especially for cooking walls. This is a Tappan design.

a dining area in or adjacent to the kitchen.

7) Ceramic tile is a beautiful and luxurious material for backsplash areas or for entire walls, although high first-cost and high installation costs often rule it out.

In Mexico, where both tile and labor are inexpensive, this bright and colorful material is used often for entire walls, floors and even ceilings. The effect is love at first sight, although the color combinations that we applaud in Mexico are usually too uninhibited for our homes in the United States.

8) Kitchen carpeting is used effectively as a wall material by many kitchen specialists. They seldom use it all the way to the ceiling (although they might if it is a large room), but they often will cove it up to the window line or up the walls of an island or peninsula. This can be done easily and inexpensively with simple flooring adhesives.

Ceilings

Kitchen ceilings, like kitchen walls, usually are painted. Paint always is adequate. It should be light colored semigloss.

The best surfacing for a kitchen ceiling is acoustical tile or sheet. It can absorb up to 70 percent of the noise striking it, and it also helps prevent kitchen noise from invading quiet areas above the kitchen.

Acoustical ceiling systems have matching lighting fixtures for clean-looking recessed installation.

The problem with acoustical tile is to get the border tiles on opposite sides of the room the same size, and as large as possible. The easy (cheap) way is simply to start at one end with full tiles and then to cut them off to the required size when the other end of the room is reached.

But instructions come with the product so it can be done properly.

There are other things that can be done with ceilings.

Kitchen carpeting can be used creatively, as can be seen in the "Successful Kitchens" illustrations elsewhere in this book.

Solid wood (or apparent solid wood) beams are often used in large kitchens, but the heir apparent to the wood beam is the polyurethane beam. It is

Armstrong's vinyl-coated Lyria Cushiontone acoustic panels have abstract pattern that conceals the acoustical perforations. This is a suspended ceiling.

totally realistic, looking exactly like wood, but it is so light that a housewife can lift it with one hand and apply it to the ceiling with adhesive.

There is the modern version of the familiar skylight, made now of clear plastic that lets in lots of daylight but eliminates some of the old leakage problems.

10

Noise Control: The Growing Need

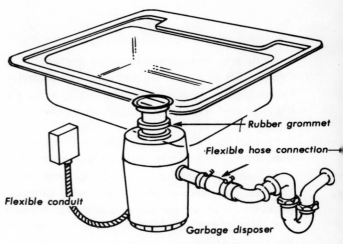

Object with disposer is to eliminate transmission of noise, isolating it in sink cabinet.

Rubber grommet

Flexible hose connection

Flexible conduit

Garbage disposer

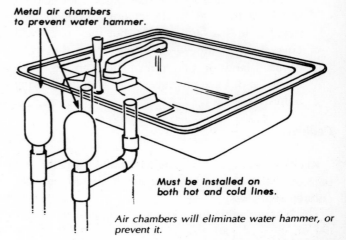

Metal air chambers to prevent water hammer.

Must be installed on both hot and cold lines.

Air chambers will eliminate water hammer, or prevent it.

A University of Wisconsin psychiatrist, Dr. J. C. Westman, has reported that "the average kitchen is like a boiler room." He blames the growing cacophony for deterioration in marriage and family life.

The effects of noise, both in the home and at work, are being studied increasingly by government, industry, and consumer groups. Not too long ago a U.S. Department of Commerce panel on noise abatement produced a preponderance of evidence that noise—independent of loudness—can degrade the quality of our lives.

Manufacturers are really doing something about it. Some disposers come with rubber mounts and rubber hose sections, and therefore, are much more quiet than others. Members of the Home Ventilating Institute have not only quieted their products but put stickers on them with their sone ratings.

The builder or remodeler can do much more, and he should, not only for the good of his customers but also for his own protection. With the growing awareness of environmental noise, standards will come. That's for sure.

Here are some of the minimums.

1) Mount the dishwasher, garbage disposer, and other appliances on pads or springs to prevent vibrations from being transmitted through the floor and countertops.
2) Wrap the sides of the dishwasher with glass fiber insulating material to prevent transmission of sound to cabinets and counter tops.
3) Use sponge rubber isolation gaskets at the mouth of the disposer to prevent the sink bowl from amplifying the grinding noise.
4) Balance the refrigerator by adjusting the set screws on the front of the unit to eliminate annoying vibration. It is balanced properly when the door closes automatically from a half-open position.
5) Place sound-absorbing mountings on the exhaust fan, and make sure the fan is large enough to operate efficiently at low speeds.
6) Install a flexible pipe, similar to an automobile radiator hose, between the drain and the trap to keep vibrations from being transmitted to other plumbing and into the walls.
7) Install pneumatic anti-hammer devices in the water lines.
8) Place rubber bushings behind cabinet doors to eliminate banging.
9) Check the drawer slides, and if they are noisy demand something better. Quiet ones are available.
10) Install an acoustical ceiling to help stifle reflected noises.

The accompanying drawings are by courtesy of Owens-Corning Fiberglas Corp.

TABLE
Home Task Area Product Generated Noise Levels*

AREA	maintains auditory attention and stimulates eye movement for localization		threshold of annoyance environment - (50 to 90dB)			airplane noises relatively unnoticed with background mus.			activates autonomic nervous system***		increase in peristalsis, saliva & gastric juice flow	annoyance threshold**	increased response and error averages over lower pressure levels / skin pales, pupils dilate, eyes close, adrenalin increases work efficiency reduced						perceptable ear discomfort human pain threshold		"feeling" sensation noticeable in ear		painful sensations
Kitchen	30	35	40	45	50	55	60	65	70	75	80	85	90	95	100	105	110	115	120	125	130	135	140
PRODUCTS*																							
Range vent fan	■	■	■	■	■	■	■	■	■	■	■	■											
Garbage disposal	■	■	■	■	■	■	■	■	■	■	■												
Dishwasher	■	■	■	■	■	■	■	■	■														
Electric mixer	■	■	■	■	■	■	■	■	■	■													
Blender	■	■	■	■	■	■	■	■	■	■	■	■	■										
Refrigerator	■	■	■	■	■																		
Wall exhaust fan	■	■	■	■	■	■	■	■	■	■	■	■	■										
12" portable fan	■	■	■	■	■	■	■	■	■														
Knife sharpener	■	■	■	■	■	■	■	■	■	■	■												

*Recorded at operator's or housewife's normal ear distance (dBA scale)
**Intermittent sounds
***Also occurs with loud or unexpected noises

Holes cut through common walls for plumbing and heating may leak noise. Seal them with a resilient material.

Koss Electronics asked the Environmental Design department of the University of Wisconsin for deep research into "The Auditory Environment in the Home" and found the kitchen is a rough equivalent of a boiler factory. Tables I and II show everything except the refrigerator is above the annoyance threshold.

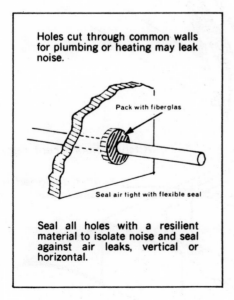

Holes cut through common walls for plumbing or heating may leak noise.

Pack with fiberglas

Seal air tight with flexible seal

Seal all holes with a resilient material to isolate noise and seal against air leaks, vertical or horizontal.

WHAT TO DO ABOUT IT:

Ventilating systems can be improved greatly by following these recommendations.

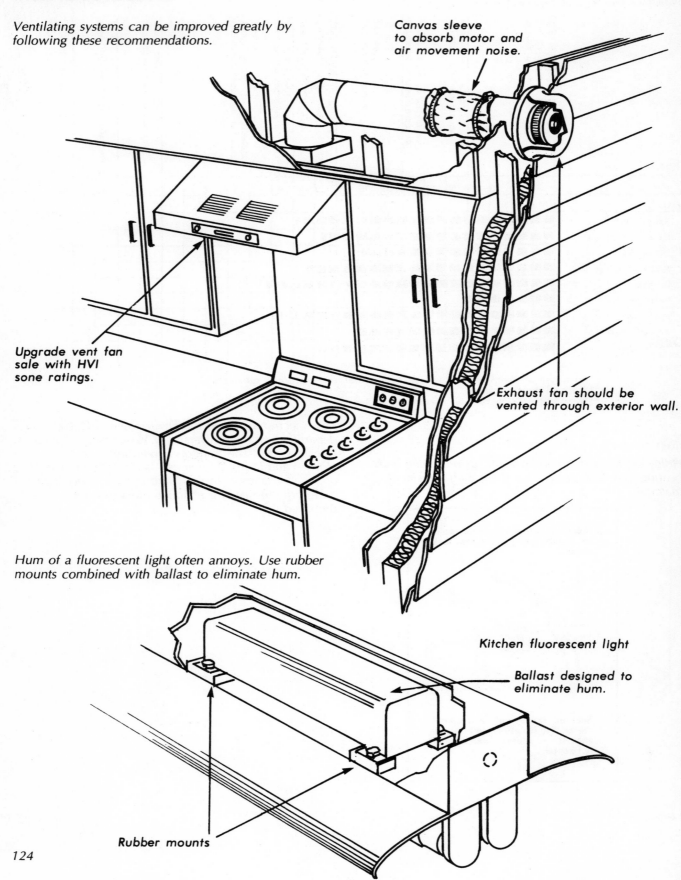

Canvas sleeve to absorb motor and air movement noise.

Upgrade vent fan sale with HVI sone ratings.

Exhaust fan should be vented through exterior wall.

Hum of a fluorescent light often annoys. Use rubber mounts combined with ballast to eliminate hum.

Kitchen fluorescent light

Ballast designed to eliminate hum.

Rubber mounts

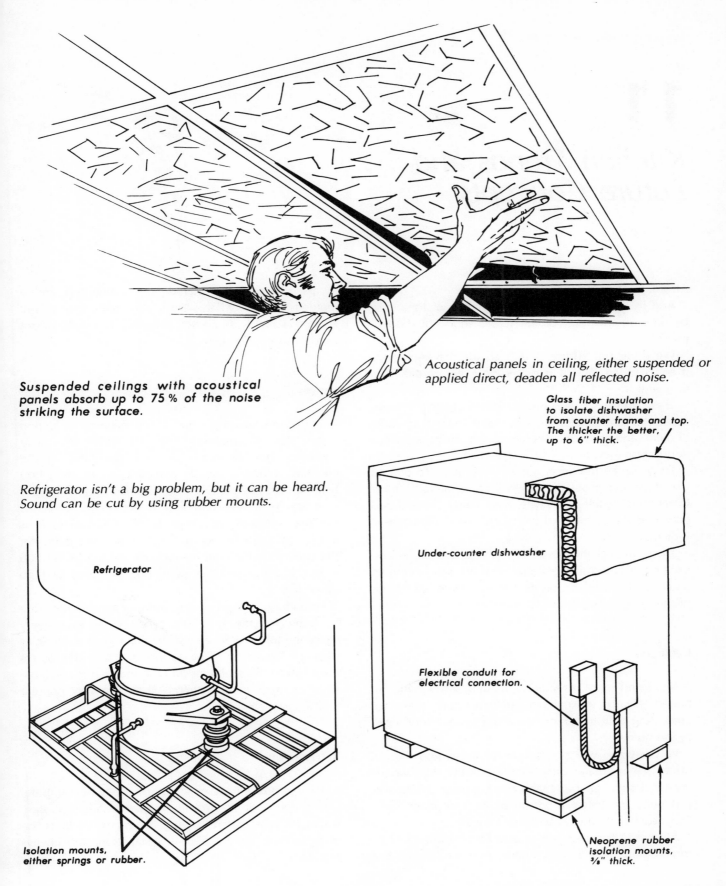

Suspended ceilings with acoustical panels absorb up to 75% of the noise striking the surface.

Acoustical panels in ceiling, either suspended or applied direct, deaden all reflected noise.

Glass fiber insulation to isolate dishwasher from counter frame and top. The thicker the better, up to 6" thick.

Refrigerator isn't a big problem, but it can be heard. Sound can be cut by using rubber mounts.

Refrigerator

Under-counter dishwasher

Flexible conduit for electrical connection.

Isolation mounts, either springs or rubber.

Neoprene rubber isolation mounts, ⅜" thick.

11

Kitchen Trends and Future Concepts

All things change.

And in the changing, will the kitchen of tomorrow become another part of the future shock of modern man?

We think not. There is a need for the kitchen as it exists today. And if it didn't exist, we would have to invent it.

There are many who predict home electronic computers for the housewife. We have looked at some of them, and no doubt they are useful. There is serious doubt, however, as to who *needs* them.

To go to the moon? Absolutely essential. To control inventory and production in a large cabinet factory? Great. But to tell your wife how many sirloins and how many cans of beans she will need next week? Ridiculous!

There are changing trends. There are new and exciting products and materials that are fast becoming parts of the kitchen of the future. Here are some of the ones to watch for.

Cabinetry

More and more, they are spreading throughout the house. Nearly all cabinet manufacturers now are promoting built-in cabinet installations for every room in the home.

Polyurethane will be popular for doors and drawer fronts. It has greater dimensional stability than wood, greater design capability, and has a greater production capability for better products at far less labor cost. Still, wood will always be in demand.

All-plastic cabinets are a possibility, built of reinforced glass fiber or polystyrene, not one by one but in assemblies which include the countertop and a molded-in sink. On this basis you might buy a 6-ft. kitchen assembly, or an 8-ft. assembly, or combinations to form L or U kitchens.

Ranges

The newest item right now is the magnetic induction system by Westinghouse. This is truly cool, safe cooking, with absolutely no heat generated in the cooktop. When a pan is placed over an induction heating coil, intercepting an oscillating magnetic field, heat results in the pan and it cooks the contents. Lift the pan and the range is off. Of course, it is a smoothtop, with not a single hole, not even for the controls, which are magnets on the top. At $2,500 it is not a mass-market item, but the price will go down fast.

Smooth, glass-top cooking surfaces are definitely the in thing for the mid-70's. They were exclusively Corning's for several years while other glass companies tried to figure out how to do it. Now the others have solved the problems and the material is available to other range manufacturers. These are very popular with consumers.

Refrigeration

The big box is neat, efficient and pretty near failsafe, but it does not fit in with modern kitchen design. It can be great when built-in, but many kitchens are budgeted too low for built-in installation, and always will be.

A better system, known for years to technologists, is a central refrigeration plant with refrigeration piped or ducted to points of use. Thus there could be cool drawers and cool cabinets in different parts of the kitchen, den, bedrooms, or where desired. If the technology is known, can the product be far behind?

Microwave

The microwave oven, first marketed by Tappan in 1955, popularized by Amana, and now brought to a peak of sophistication by Thermador really belongs in every home above poverty level.

It has survived the radiation scare (it is about as dangerous as sunlight) and now is within reach of anyone with a credit card. As more wives join the work force, the need for this fast-cooking appliance increases. When both husband and wife get home from work at 5:30 or 6, a regular, conventional family meal is easily possible through the wonders of microwave. This product will become really big through the mid-70s.

Countertops

High-pressure plastic laminates may finally be challenged by the new cast marbles (synthetic, polyester or acrylic) and by a new material being developed by Corning.

The latter is Pyram, a thin surfacing material applied to a substrate but with the characteristics of Pyroceram, which is the material Corning uses for its glass-ceramic cooktops and counter inserts.

This possibly will not be a serious challenge for the plastic laminates, but in the ever-expanding marketplace there is more and more room for new materials, and they do have their points.

Fractional Kitchens

These are the bits of kitchens scattered through the house. There will be more of them. Compact refrigerators already are selling profusely for offices, and that engenders ideas.

At home they are popping up in bedrooms, dens, and recreation rooms. With them frequently goes a

Is there a computer in our future? At $10,600 we doubt if this will show up in any HUD housing, but here it is, by Honeywell. In the price you get a 2-week course in programming for such things as menu-planning, home budgeting and income tax computation. Fiberglas components are made for Honeywell by Wehco Plastics, West Trenton, N.J.

wet bar, which means bar sink with running water and cabinets, possibly even a microwave oven.

The industry makes unit kitchens, or compact kitchens, incorporating a small oven, sink, refrigerator, and one or two burners in as little as 19 inches of wall space. These usually are constructed of steel and are too commercial looking for a home. The fractional kitchens now showing up in homes are designed and made up for a particular place in the home.

This "Homemaker's Command Post" by
Westinghouse includes closed circuit TV on all of the
house. Telephone has 500 names and numbers stored
in memory bank. She can unlock doors and windows
by touching a button, or lock them, or a button will
call firemen or police. It's in the Electra 71 home
in Coral Springs, Fla.

Elkay conceptualizes this visionary sink of the future,
its Cuisine 80. It combines all sink functions—food
preparation, cooking and cleanup, plus closed-circuit
TV, and, of course, a small computer.

The Cabinet-Appliance

Back in the early 1950s Remington Rand developed
an automated filing cabinet for its office equipment
division, called the Cardveyor.

Now it has been brought up to date as a kitchen
appliance—automated storage space that brings the
various bins of foods, dishes or pans at the press
of a button.

It costs around $2,000 to a builder or dealer. It
replaces several hundred dollars worth of cabinets and,
although it is bulky, it can gain space if engineered
into the floorplan properly.

This automated cabinet-appliance might be combined with a dumb waiter, bringing selected shelves
from their storage spaces in the basement and thereby
releasing much space in the living area of the home.
It may never happen, but it is not difficult to imagine.

Other Gadgetry

Built in intercom systems are sophisticated and highly
useful. They can be wired to as many rooms in the
house as desired, and the deluxe ones include fire
and burglar alarms and even phonographs.

Closed-circuit television can be a great thing for
mother working in the kitchen. Covering the backyard
play area it can be much more useful and convenient
than the window in the kitchen, and it also can cover
upstairs or downstairs play areas. The coming age
of home videotaping has ramifications that can only
be suggested.

The world is full of super-kitchen visions of the
future, but it is not our purpose here to discuss them.
We speak here of what exists, what is imminent, or
what is both possible and logical. And so it isn't
unrealistic to say this is the way it is going to be.

Range of the future may use magnetic induction for really cool cooking. This, by Westinghouse, is available now and boiling water through a kitchen towel proves that cool means cool. Full view shows that it is a glass-top, with absolutely no holes for dirt to get in. Even the controls are magnetic. They slide along in their proper places, and can be picked up for cleaning. Its principle: oscillating magnetic field creates similar field when it encounters resistance of metal cooking vessel. This causes heat in pan, not on cooktop, causing food to cook.

Members, Council of Certified Kitchen Designers

The only measure of true professionalism in kitchen design and planning is recognition of an individual as a Certified Kitchen Designer by the certifying arm of the American Institute of Kitchen Dealers. Certification is awarded only after a minimum number of years in the field with extensive testing and affidavits from customers.

There are many other good kitchen designers and planners who cannot win CKD recognition because they do not have the required years of experience. Others choose not to be certified.

The following list of Certified Kitchen Designers provides a nationwide list of design and planning sources. In any local area, an alternative would be to look for a kitchen firm that is a member of AIKD. In many cities these are listed in the yellow pages with the AIKD logotype.

Arizona

A. M. Buck, CKD, Crowe Lumber & Construction Co., 1445 E. Indian School Road, Phoenix, 85014

California

M. D. Mitchell, CKD, Carefree Kitchens Inc., 241 S. Euclid St., Anaheim, 92802

J. B. Galloway, CKD, H. H. Holbrook Kitchens & Baths, 1680 Tustin Av., Costa Mesa, 92627

C. A. Olson, CKD, Downey Plumbing & Heating Co., 11829 So. Downey Avenue, Downey, 90241

J. N. Coppes, CKD, 720 Ramage St., Los Angeles, 90069

R. K. Crossman, CKD, S. California Gas Co., Box 3249, Los Angeles, 90051

S. M. Macey, CKD, Quesco Cabinets, Inc., 829 So. Claremont Street, San Mateo, 94402

W. E. Peterson, CKD, 3018 Third St., Santa Monica, 90405

C. W. Todd, CKD, Safeway Construction Co., 18801 Crenshaw Blvd., Torrance, 90503

Colorado

W. B. Jordan, CKD, Jordan's, Inc., 121 E. Bijou, Colorado Springs, 80902

E. Hanley, CKD, Edward Hanley & Company, 1448 Oneida Street, Denver, 80220

P. G. Hartman, CKD, Kitchen Distributors, Inc., 1235 South Broadway, Denver, 80210

C. W. Kline, CKD, Bill Kline Kitchens, 2640 E. 3rd Avenue, Denver, 80206

H. H. Schmidt, CKD, Kitchen Distributors Inc., 1235 S. Broadway, Denver, 80210

B. H. Smith, CKD, Vent-A-Hood of Denver, Inc., 20 East Ninth Avenue, Denver, 80203

Connecticut

G. H. Mann, CKD, Ralph Mann & Sons, 505 Main Street, Ansonia, 06401

A. Kasper, CKD, K. L. & P. Kitchens, 4173 Main Street, Bridgeport, 06606

A. S. Audibert, CKD, Audibert's, 781 King Street, Bristol, 06010

J. K. Metzo, CKD, Metzo Bros., Inc., 334 Main Street, East Haven, 06512

G. D. Crane, CKD, Paul Dolan Co., Inc., Essex, 06426

L. J. Kowalski, CKD, W. R. Penney, CKD, Kowalski's, Inc., 202 Field Point Road, Greenwich, 06830

R. L. Gelormino, CKD, F. P. Palmer, CKD, Kustom Kitchens of Litchfield, Inc., Torrington Road, Litchfield, 06759

K. L. Bell, CKD, Bell Kitchen Distributors, Inc., 363 Mulberry Street, P.O. Box 12, Plantsville, 06479

E. C. Brady, CKD, G. I. Greaves, CKD, Kitchens of Distinction by Brady, 90 Center Street, Southington, 06489

E. L. Chadwick, CKD, Living Kitchens, Inc., 896 Washington Boulevard, Stamford, 06901

D. L. Davis, CKD, Bradley Kitchens, Inc., 214 Park Road, West Hartford, 06119

B. O. Peterson, CKD, R. C. Aldridge, CKD, M. A. Peterson, CKD, M. A. Peterson, Inc., 607 New Park Avenue, West Hartford, 06110

S. M. Lefler, CKD, Kitchens by Lefler, 431 East State Street, Westport, 06880

Delaware

W. G. Magan, CKD, R. Walls, CKD, Craft-Way Kitchens, Inc., Evelyn Drive at Kirkwood Highway, Wilmington, 19808

District of Columbia

A. R. Dresner, CKD, Douglas Distributing Corporation, 3521 ''V'' Street N.E., Washington, 20018

R. W. Bauer, CKD, R. D. Schafer, CKD, The Kitchen Guild, 5002 Connecticut Avenue N.W., Washington, 20008

L. E. Schucker, Jr., CKD, L. E. Schucker, III, CKD, B. J. Scoby, CKD, Kitchens, Inc., 5027 Connecticut Avenue N.W., Washington, 20008

Florida

R. L. Welky, CKD, Mutschler Kitchens of Fort Lauderdale, 233 Southeast Second Avenue, Fort Lauderdale, 33301

R. F. Braithwaite, CKD, House of Wares, Inc., 2975 N.W. 77 Avenue, Miami, 33122

R. V. Kucera, CKD, Kitchen Center, Inc., 5124 Biscayne Boulevard, Miami, 33137

G. A. Nunnally, CKD, Benchmark Cabinetry, 4308 NE 2nd Av., Miami, 33137

W. T. Langohr, CKD, Ocean Reef Club, North Key Largo, 33037

F. B. Schone, CKD, Mutschler Kitchens, 610 Prosperity Farms Rd., North Palm Beach, 33408

F. D. Kay, CKD, Direct, Inc., 2911 N. Palafox, Pensacola, 32502

L. E. Miller, CKD, 4119 Zeller St., Tampa, 33609

Georgia

G. C. Mays, CKD, A. H. Snelling, Jr., CKD, J. B. Bennett, CKD, Custom Kitchens Co., 808 W. Oglethorpe Avenue, Albany 31701

P. B. Gunter, CKD, Marblecast, Inc., 1415 Chattahoochee Avenue, Atlanta, 30318

R. E. Mayer, CKD, Perspective Drawing Service, Rte. 1, Mt. Tabor Rd., Dallas, 30132

Hawaii

M. L. Smith, CKD, Ramsay Contractors, 630 Piikoi Street, Honolulu, 96814

Illinois

E. J. Keegan, CKD, Key Kitchens, 1628 W. Northwest Highway, Arlington Heights, 60004

R. W. Lautz, CKD, V. P. Schifferdecker, CKD, Schifferdecker Kitchens, 3712 W. Main St., Belleville, 62223

L. S. Colbert, CKD, M. R. Stalter, CKD, Colberts, 1602 South Neil Street, Champaign, 61820

C. L. Anderson, CKD, Kitchen Shoppe Inc., 5001-03 W. Irving Park Road, Chicago, 60641

B. G. Greenwald, CKD, Suburban Designers, Inc., 2412 West 111th Street, Chicago, 60655

G. A. Reilly, CKD, People's Gas Co., 122 S. Michigan Avenue, Chicago, 60603

J. C. Turkstra, CKD, Turkstra's Modernizing Center, 10958 S. Halsted St., Chicago, 60628

V. M. Stratton, CKD, American Kitchen Designs, 804 W. Main St., Collinsville, 62234

G. E. Coutant, CKD, Kitchen Distributors, 1449 East Eldorado, Decatur, 62521

L. C. Rice, CKD, J. J. Swartz Co., 2120 N. Oakland Av., Decatur, 62526

R. V. Mueller, CKD, Edwardsville Lumber Co., 201 W. High, Edwardsville, 62025

D. A. Rohrberg, CKD, Beemer Enterprises, 657 E. 2nd St., El Paso, 61738

C. H. Seeds, CKD, Design Associates, 115 E. Stephenson, Freeport, 61032

B. G. Stidman, CKD, Galatia Building Center, Box 127, Galatia, 62935

S. C. Gilfoyle, CKD, Creative Interiors, 233 N. Commerce St., Galena, 61036

R. P. Gerth, CKD, Geneva Industries, Inc., 201 S. 8th Street, Geneva, 60134

J. P. Descour, CKD, Town & Country Kitchens, Inc., 712 Glencoe Road, Glencoe, 60022

R. W. Loerop, CKD, Loerop Co., 8100 S. County Line Rd., Hinsdale, 60521

D. Johnson, CKD, Kitchens by Don Johnson, 17930 Dixie Highway, Homewood, 60430

E. L. Johnson, CKD, Mutschler Bros., 595 E. Illinois Rd., Lake Forest, 60045

K. Miller, CKD, Kitchens & Baths by Kenneth Miller, 18 West 664 Roosevelt Road, Lombard, 60148

L. R. Svendson, CKD, Les Svendson & Associates, Rte. 3, Box 228, Long Grove, 60047

G. A. Reilly, CKD, 148 S. Lake St., Mundelein, 60060

E. L. Zielinski, CKD, Better Kitchens, Inc., 7640 Milwaukee Avenue, Niles, 60648

R. P. Junghans, CKD, The Building Specialties Co., Tucker Beach Road, Paris, 61944

A. G. Ackerberg Jr., CKD, Ideal Millwork Co., Rt. 1, Box 103, Plainfield, 60544

W. A. Reynolds Jr., CKD, Howard Sersen, CKD, Reynolds Enterprises, 2936 River Rd., River Grove, 60171

F. W. Eber, CKD, Eber's of Rochelle, 426 N. 11th Street, Rochelle, 61068

O. R. Beardsley, CKD, R. O. Geddes, CKD, R. J. Rogers, CKD, L. P. Thompson, CKD, St. Charles Mfg. Co., 1611 E. Main St., St. Charles, 60174

M. A. Dummler, CKD, J. A. Kathrein, CKD, Totem Lumber Co., 4421 Ruby Street, Schiller Park, 60176

M. H. Braun, CKD, R. J. Kansy, CKD, Mark Braun Kitchens, 1805 S. MacArthur, Springfield, 62704

H. R. Buckhold, CKD, McDermand Kitchens, 1831 So. 11th Street, Springfield, 62703

K. G. Knobel, CKD, K. P. Knobel, CKD, Karl G. Knobel, Inc., 1218 Washington Avenue, Wilmette, 60091

Indiana

R. E. Nichols, CKD, Cabinets by Nichols, Box 311, Bargersville, 46106

R. S. Penrod, CKD, Penn Kitchens, 313 East Third Street, Bloomington, 47401

L. G. Routen, CKD, The Kitchen Center, Corner Eleventh & Rogers, Bloomington, 47401

L. W. Alexander, CKD, Dunlap's, 422 Washington Street, Columbus, 47201

A. L. Skomp, CKD, C. E. Skomp, CKD, Cliff's Napanee Kitchens, 1415 E. Division Street, Evansville, 47714

J. M. Boarman, CKD, Boarman Cabinet Co., 1627 Oliver Avenue, Indianapolis, 46221

C. L. Gray, Jr., CKD, Gray-Breese Co., 3750 W. 16th Street, Indianapolis, 46222

A. Raup, CKD, Raup's, 5343 Keystone Av., Indianapolis, 46220

C. P. Pippen, CKD, Pippens Kitchens, Inc., 428 N. Washington Street, Muncie, 47305

R. E. Chapman, CKD, Coppes Inc., Nappanee, 46550

D. P. Guckenberger, CKD, E. L. Johnson, CKD, R. S. Ringenberg, CKD, Mutschler Bros. Co., 302 S. Madison Street, Nappanee, 46550

J. D. Mitchell, CKD, Kitchen Interiors, R. R. 3 Box 6, Newburg, 47630

R. John, CKD, Foust Lumber & Building Supplies, 402 N. 14th St., New Castle, 47362

V. A. Wietbrock, CKD, Koremen Co., 2142 U.S. 41, Schererville, 46375

C. A. Berg, CKD, House of Kitchens, 737 Ewing St., Seymour, 47274

J. L. Risley, CKD, Risley's Kitchen Specialists, 212 East Broadway, Shelbyville, 46176

D. E. Carpenter, CKD, Carpenter Enterprises, 3710 Surrey Lane, South Bend, 46628

W. M. Beemer, CKD, Beemer Enterprises, Inc., R.R. #1, Syracuse, 46567

W. F. Frazier, CKD, Frazier, Distr. Co., Inc., Kitchens & Interior Designs, 1318 Ohio Street, Terre Haute, 47807

Iowa

W. C. Fox, CKD, Fox Appliance & Kitchen Center, Inc., 705–11 Jefferson Street, Burlington, 52601

W. T. Gerdes, CKD, Benson Lumber Co., 1207 Lucas Avenue, Burlington, 52601

W. M. Hoffman, CKD, Keystone Products Co., 2880 Mt. Pleasant Street, Burlington, 52601

H. R. Ek, CKD, F. B. Friedl, CKD, St. Charles Kitchens by Friedl, Inc., 1013 Mt. Vernon Road, S.E., Cedar Rapids, 52403

O. F. Maxwell, CKD, Brammer Mfg. Co., 1701 Rockingham Road, Davenport, 52808

G. E. Nordeen, CKD, Nordeen's Home Supply Co., 314 E. 2nd Street, Davenport, 52801

A. A. Johnson, CKD, Kitchen Center, Inc., 5055 Second Avenue, Des Moines, 50333

C. Swanson, CKD, Swanson's Kitchens, 1505 Fremont Street, Marshalltown, 50158

F. H. Thompson, CKD, Thompson & Associates, Inc., 1st & Ashworth Road, West Des Moines, 50265

Kentucky

D. M. Butcher, CKD, Creative Kitchens, Inc., 1269 Eastland Drive, Lexington, 40505

R. B. Cornett, CKD, Kitchen Planning Center, 316 N. Ashland Av., Lexington, 40502

F. R. Smith, CKD, Kitchen Planning Center, 101 W. Loudan, Lexington, 40508

W. J. Ketcham, CKD, L. T. Allen, CKD, J. U. Forst, CKD, C. J. Mattingly, CKD, General Electric Co., Appliance Park, Bldg. 4, Room 216, Louisville, 40225

P. M. Pittenger, CKD, The House of Kitchens, Inc., 106 Bauer Avenue, Louisville, 40207

J. W. Riley, Jr., CKD, Jefferson Kitchens, Inc., 1034 Rogers Street, Louisville, 40204

Louisiana

C. B. Gamble, CKD, Kitchens by Cameron, Inc., 8019 Palm Street, New Orleans, 70125

Maine

C. Bellegarde, Jr., CKD, P. Clifford, CKD, R. O. Dion, CKD, Bellegarde Custom Kitchens, 516 Sabattus Street, Lewiston, 04240

Maryland

R. F. Cox, CKD, R. L. Gibbs, CKD, Cox Kitchens & Baths Inc., 5011 York Road, Baltimore, 21212

C. G. Neubauer Jr., CKD, AAA Remodeling Co., 2907 Taylor Avenue, Baltimore, 21234

A. V. Taylor, CKD, Taylor's Kitchens, 2214 E. Monument Street, Baltimore, 21205

B. Kirk, CKD, Kitchen Fair, 417 S. Highland Av., Baltimore, 21224

J. S. Bendheim, CKD, Builder Kitchens Inc., 10710 Tucker St., Beltsville, 20705

R. M. Tunis, CKD, 7032 Wisconsin Av., Bethesda, 20015

D. S. Wheelhouse, CKD, Murray Saunders Custom Kitchens, Inc., 4918 Bethesda Avenue, Bethesda, 20014

P. V. Chadik, CKD, Mutschler-Division of American Standard, 2920 Greenvale Road, Chevy Chase, 20015

A. W. Neumann, Jr., CKD, Ann Dor Kitchens, Route 140 & Sandymount Road, Finksburg, 21048

R. L. Alexander, CKD, Gaithersburg Lumber & Supply Co., Inc., 11 S. Frederick Avenue, Gaithersburg, 20760

J. Dobbs, CKD, N. Granat, CKD, Creative Kitchens, Inc., 8480 Fenton Place, Silver Spring, 20910

H. E. Fowler, CKD, Waldorf Supply, Inc., Md. Route #5, Waldorf, 20601

Massachusetts

R. T. Arnold Jr., CKD, Arnold's 1788 Yards Inc., 44 Spring Street, Adams, 01220

J. Herzenberg, CKD, Kitchens by Herzenberg, Inc., South End Bridge Circle, Agawam, 01001

L. K. Johnson, CKD, Lee Kimball Kitchens, 119 Canal Street, Boston, 02114

S. F. Brown, CKD, Brown's Kitchen & Bath Center, 56 N. Putnam St., Danvers, 01923

T. J. Pitkanen, CKD, Boyd Craft, Inc., 62 Walnut Street, Dedham, 02026

F. R. Angel, CKD, The Angel Co., Inc., 340 Broad Street, Fitchburg, 01420

R. W. Burke, CKD, Kitchen Center of Framingham, Inc., 697 Waverly Street, Framingham, 01701

V. M. Gallivan, CKD, Colonial Floors, Inc., Kitchen Division, 117 Waverly Street, Framingham, 01701

R. L. Norberg, CKD, Suburban Kitchens, 1242 Hyde Park Avenue, Hyde Park, 02136

R. G. Peckham, CKD, Peckham's Custom Kitchens, 155 Park St., New Bedford, 02740

N. E. Robitaille, CKD, Tailored Kitchens Supply Co., 100 Tarkiln Hill Road, New Bedford, 02745

L. S. Gagliardi, CKD, Gagliardi's, Inc., 9-13 Union Street, North Adams, 01247

H. W. Watkins, CKD, Nickerson Lumber Co., 51 Main Street, Orleans, 02653

W. H. Gustafson, CKD, The Kitchen Center, Route 146, Sutton, 01527

H. C. Hjelm, CKD, Architectural Woodworking Co., Inc., 241 West Boylston Street, West Boylston, 01583

B. F. Rice, CKD, W. E. Rice, CKD, Kitchens by Rice Bros., Inc., 3 R Church Street, Wilmington, 01887

J. T. Margrabia Jr., CKD, Jo-Mar Corp., 7 Spruce St., Winchester, 01890

J. F. Boyer, CKD, Sawyer's, Gold Star Blvd., Worcester, 01606

R. A. Cuccaro, CKD, Robert A. Cuccaro Associates, 6 Alvarado Avenue, Worcester, 01604

Michigan

R. S. Pleune, CKD, Croswell Kitchens, Jordan Sheperd Inc., 517 Ada Dr. SE, Ada, 49301

D. J. Thibodeau, CKD, Home Appliance Mart, Inc., 2019 W. Stadium Blvd., Ann Arbor, 48103

W. M. Weinlander Jr., CKD, Weinlander Wood Products & Home Supply, Inc., 8593 E. U.S. 223, Blissfield, 49228

B. J. Maday, CKD, Maday Kitchens Inc., 7483 Dixie Hwy., Bridgeport, 48722

D. N. Street, CKD, White Supply Co., 639 E. Chicago Road, Coldwater, 49036

J. R. Allcorn, CKD, Artistan Plastic, Inc., 12001 Greenfield, Detroit, 48227

C. E. Clark, CKD, Charlotte Clark Kitchens, 18932 W. McNichols Road, Detroit, 48219

J. M. Damstra, CKD, Gallery of Kitchens, 5243 Plainfield N.E., Grand Rapids, 49505

C. A. Kosmalski, CKD, Mutschler Kitchens, Inc., 20227 Mack Avenue, Grosse Pointe Woods, 48236

D. C. Nicholson, CKD, The Kitchen Shop, Inc., 407 1st Street, Jackson, 49201

R. E. Paspas, CKD, Capitol City Lumber Co., 700 E. Kalamazoo St., Lansing, 48904

M. E. Blake, CKD, R. A. Ferle, CKD, The Kitchen Shop, Inc., 5320 S. Pennsylvania, Lansing, 48910

R. B. Vandervoort, CKD, Hager-Fox Co., 1115 S. Pennsylvania Ave., Lansing, 48920

R. E. Hill, CKD, Style Trend Kitchens, 792 W. Laketon Avenue, Muskegon, 49441

L. E. Trevarrow Jr., CKD, Trevarrow, Inc., 23712 Woodward Avenue, Pleasant Ridge, 48069

C. Pajares, CKD, Pajares Construction Products, Inc., 2680 S. Rochester Rd., Rochester, 48063

R. E. Holton, CKD, Royal Oak Kitchens Inc., 4518 N. Woodward Royal Oak, 48072

F. B. Terpstra, CKD, Southfield Kitchens, 22050 W. Ten Mile Road, Southfield, 48075

L. G. Fogelsong, CKD, R. L. Fogelsong, CKD, Tecumseh Building Supply Co., 214 E. Chicago Blvd., Tecumseh, 49286

Minnesota

H. M. Eberhart, CKD, Dura Supreme, Inc., 10710 County Road 15, Minneapolis, 55427

Mississippi

J. P. Campbell, CKD, Campbell Co., Inc., 2022 25 Avenue, Gulfport, 39501

Missouri

S. C. Keck, CKD, Heart of the Home Kitchens, West Ely Rd., Hannibal, 63401

D. B. Cole, CKD, Kitchens by Cole, Hwy 54, Osage Beach, 65065

A. Baum, CKD, J. Baum, CKD, The Kitchen Shop, Inc., 1063 S. Brentwood Blvd., St. Louis, 63117

W. C. Karr, CKD, Kitchens by Karr, 8456 Watson Rd., St. Louis, 63119

C. J. Polley, CKD, Coppes, Inc., 5040 A Devonshire, St. Louis, 63109

Montana

J. W. Bergeson, CKD, W. A. Shaffer, CKD, Modern Kitchens, Inc., P.O. Box 1881, 2710 Montana Avenue, Billings, 59103

New Hampshire

J. L. Brown, CKD, R. C. Elliot, CKD, Home Improvement Co., Inc., Meriden Road, Lebanon, 03766

J. R. Higgins, CKD, J. R. Higgins, Inc., 449 Hayward Street, Manchester, 03103

J. Mitrook, CKD, Mitrook's Custom Kitchen Center, 100 Albany Street P.O. Box 1152, Portsmouth, 03801

New Jersey

D. P. Pietruszka, CKD, J. F. Pietruszka, CKD, Woodward Kitchens, 37 Linnet St., Bayonne, 07002

W. J. Kelly, CKD, Kitchen Creations by Kelly, Div. of Smith & Richards Lumber Co., 110 South Laurel Street, Bridgeton, 08302

A. E. Rosner, CKD, M. Rosner, CKD, Rosner's Custom Kitchens, 1700 W. Marlton Pike, Cherry Hill, 08034

A. J. Giannaula, CKD, Allied Woodcraft, 421 Allwood Road, Clifton, 07012

C. A. Schneider, CKD, C. Schneider & Co., Inc., 158-166 Highland Avenue, Clifton, 07011

W. Begbie, CKD, Begbie's Kitchens, Inc., Route 46, Dover, 07801

V. R. Loretto, CKD, Allied Craftsman, 409 E. Madison Av., Dumont, 07628

J. P. Castronova, CKD, Paramount Kitchens, 211 Central Avenue, East Newark, 07029

L. Lemchen, CKD, Barmark, Inc., 198 Central Avenue, East Orange, 07018

G. C. Murphy, CKD, Kitchen Masters Inc., 100 Rte. 46, E. Paterson, 07407

M. E. Dudick, CKD, 40 North Av., Garwood, 07027

R. W. Afflerbach, CKD, L. P. Scarani, CKD, AIKD, 114 Main St., Hackettstown, 07840

J. Van Beuzekom, CKD, T. J. Bogusta, CKD, Van Beuzekom Kitchens Inc., 301 Lafayette Av., Hawthorne, 07506

W. H. Bryce, CKD, Hawthorne Kitchens Inc., Fifth & Utter Av., Hawthorne, 07506

M. A. Waimon, CKD, 4 Dawson Terrace, Livingston, 07039

C. J. Curtis, CKD, H. M. Forvour, CKD, Curtis Styled Kitchens, Rt. 39 & Rudderow Avenue, Maple Shade, 08052

A. Kessler, CKD, J. A. Yesbek, CKD, Paterson Stove & Kitchen Center, 88 Broadway, Paterson, 07505

T. E. Lutjen, CKD, Jeffreys & Lutjen Inc., 29 Evans Pl., Pompton Plains, 07444

E. M. Peresett, CKD, Peresett Appliance Sales & Service, 875 State Rd., Princeton, 08540

H. Aulert Jr., CKD, G. E. Fross, CKD, Kitchen Planning & Design Center, 29 E. Milton Avenue, Rahway, 07065

J. D. Ulrich, CKD, P. W. Fluhr, CKD, Ulrich, Inc., 100 Chestnut Street, Ridgewood, 07450

P. E. Horvath, CKD, G. C. Horvath, CKD, Proven Design, Inc., 111 E. Westfield Avenue, Roselle Park, 07204

C. A. Bothers, CKD, A. R. Bothers Woodworking, Inc., 236 Dukes Pky. P.O. Box 127, Somerville, 08876

L. Shur, CKD, H. B. Sobel, CKD, Builders Fair, Inc., 22 Rt. 22, Springfield, 07081

T. Davis, CKD, Quaker Maid Kitchens by Davis, Inc., 53 Route 33, Trenton, 08619

M. Salinard, CKD, B. R. Tunbridge, CKD, Du-Craft, Inc., 1919 Rt. 71, West Belmar, 07719

G. G. Hurwitz, CKD, A. J. Terragrossa, CKD, Quaker Maid Kitchens of Haddon Twp., Inc., 108 Haddon Avenue, Westmont, 08108

J. L. Whittaker, CKD, Jay L. Whittaker Co., Inc., 15 Bergenline Avenue, Westwood, 07675

New York

F. J. Schneider, CKD, Cox Kitchens, Inc., 1163 Willis Avenue, Albertston, 11507

H. R. Myers, CKD, H. R. Myers Lumber Co., Inc., Box 147 Route 12, Boonville, 13309

J. L. Langan, CKD, Kitchen Fashions Inc., 2738 Atlantic Av., Brooklyn, 11207

J. L. Clouser, CKD, Clouser Sales, Inc., Rt. 32, Cornwall, 12518

A. Cohen, CKD, Alamode Kitchen Center, 110-29 Horace Harding Blvd., Corona, 11368

A. J. Scott, CKD, Whitehall Cabinets, Inc., 21 Ryder Place, East Rockaway, 11518

L. J. Ryder, CKD, Ryder's Kitchen & Appliances, Inc., 2026 Lake Street, Elmira, 14903

N. Papaceno, CKD, Karpy Kitchens, Rte. 17A, Florida, 10921

F. M. Frank, CKD, T. L. Frank, CKD, Alamode Kitchen Center, Inc., 2272 Jericho Tpke., Garden City Park, 11530

M. Berkoff, CKD, B. Bisulk, CKD, H. P. Bisulk, CKD, Herbert P. Bisulk, Inc., 295 Nassau Blvd., Garden City South, 11530

F. P. Frederick, CKD, H. Jacoby, CKD, Frederick Construction Co., 79-49 Myrtle Avenue, Glendale, 11227

R. J. Dorey, CKD, Finch Pruyn Sales, Inc., Quaker & Glenwood Ave., Glens Falls, 12801

D. C. Tait, CKD, Dan Tait, Inc., Grand Gorge, 12434

C. Mustello Jr., CKD, D & M Kitchens, Inc., 400 Great Neck Road, Great Neck, 11021

E. E. Berger, CKD, Berger Appliances, 441 Commerce Street, Hawthorne, 10532

C. T. Passaro, CKD, Whitehall Kitchen Center, 1231 Station Plaza, Hewlett, 11557

J. M. Kennedy, Jr., CKD, R. F. Kennedy, CKD, Kennedy Kitchens, Inc., 727 Fox Street, Horseheads, 14845

R. M. Baker, Jr., CKD, Bob Baker's Kitchens, 401 E. State Street, Ithaca, 14850

S. Y. Adams, CKD, R. F. Carbrey, CKD, Valley Crafts, Inc., Valley Plaza, Johnson City, 13790

E. M. Soper, CKD, Soper Cabinet & Fixture Co., Inc., 26-28 Downs Street, Kingston, 12401

C. R. Spetts, CKD, Charm Kitchens by Spetts, Commercial Drive, Route 5A, New Hartford, 13413

Frank Berg, CKD, R. W. Baum, CKD, Berg & Brown, 1390 Lexington Av., New York City, 10028

R. J. Brady, CKD, General Electric Co., 205 East 42nd Street, New York City, 10017

F. E. Drucker, CKD, Fred E. Drucker & Associates, Inc., 853 Lexington Avenue, New York City, 10021

I. Schwartz, CKD, Bakit Industries, Inc., 32 East 30th Street, New York City, 10016

F. A. Tommasini, CKD, Kitchen & Bath Ind., 1179 Rte. 58, New York City, 10019

J. F. Werner, CKD, Werner Associates, Inc., 136 East 74th Street, New York City, 10021

E. M. Scardaccione, CKD, Lee Appliance Inc., Rte 3, Plattsburgh, 12901

D. L. Thomas, CKD, D. L. Thomas Heating & Plumbing, Outer Market Street, Potsdam, 13676

J. C. Ferrara, CKD, Joseph O. Ferrara & Sons Inc., 125-01 Liberty Av., Richmond Hill, 11419

F. Thayer, Jr., CKD, St. Charles of Western New York, Inc., 1400 E. Henrietta Road, Rochester, 14623

I. Taras, CKD, Art-Craft Kitchens, Inc., 144 Sunrise Highway, Rockville Centre, 11570

J. D. Opper, CKD, Opper's Custom Kitchens, 186 W. Dominick, Rome, 13440

C. J. Arzonetti, CKD, Garth Custom Kitchens, Inc., 24 Garth Road, Scarsdale, 10583

R. A. Anderson, CKD, R. A. Anderson & Co., 77 Lincoln St., Staten Island, 10306

C. Van Name, CKD, Staten Island Woodworking Co., Inc., 1475 Hylan Boulevard, Staten Island, 10305

B. M. Kolner, CKD, Kolner Kitchens, 100 Edward St., Schenectady, 12304

H. Horowitz, CKD, R. Horowitz, CKD, H.R.H. Designs Inc., Box 158, Selkirk, 12158

D. J. Zieno, CKD, Sidney Appliance & Modern Kitchens, 89 Main St., Sidney, 13838

R. F. Martino, CKD, Modern Kitchens of Syracuse, Inc., 2380 Erie Blvd. East, Syracuse, 13224

A. Miller, CKD, J. J. Miller, CKD, Mid-State Kitchens, 351 5th Av., Troy, 12182

A. Gulbis, CKD, E. Gulbis, CKD, Lifetime Kitchens, Inc., 269 Columbus Avenue, Tuckahoe, 10707

D. D'Anna, CKD, Danark Associates Inc., 78 Rockaway Av., Valley Stream, 11580

W. H. Algier, CKD, Empire Kitchen & Woodworking, Inc., 862 South Road, Wappingers Falls, 12590

R. A. Coons, CKD, R. C. Supply, Warnerville & Mineral Springs Rd., Warnerville, 12187

J. A. Barth, CKD, 306 Ayer Road, Williamsville, 14221

S. B. Wechter, CKD, Sidney B. Wechter Corp., 30 Hillside Av., Williston Park, 11596

North Carolina

R. D. Finlayson, CKD, Kitchen Creations of Charlotte, 130 West Boulevard, Charlotte, 28203

F. C. Stahl, CKD, IXL Furniture Co., Rte. 1, Elizabeth City, 27909

S. E. Holt, CKD, Cape Fear Supply Co., 319 W. Russell St., Fayetteville, 28302

P. B. Gunter, CKD, Standard Supply Co. Inc., 2512 Yonkers Rd., Raleigh, 27604

North Dakota

D. W. Smith, CKD, Cabinets, Inc., 2600 Main Avenue, P.O. Box 626, Fargo, 58102

Ohio

H. S. Hembury, CKD, Tailormade Kitchen Co., 1063 S. Arlington Street, Akron, 44306

C. G. Schweikert, CKD, Schweikert Bros. Kitchens, 361 W. North Street, Akron, 44303

F. A. Valentine, CKD, Williams Kitchens, 5308 Fulton Drive N.W., Canton, 44718

R. E. Bolte, CKD, Bolte Home Improvement Co., 9526 Winton Road, Cincinnati, 45231

R. P. Halpin, CKD, Kitchens by Nickoson, 3511 Harrison Avenue, Cincinnati, 45211

R. E. Klein, CKD, Kustom Kitchens by Klein, 4342 Harrison Avenue, Cincinnati, 45211

J. F. Rugh, CKD, Valley Floor Covering Co., 417 Wyoming Avenue, Cincinnati, 45215

M. P. Daily, CKD, A. G. Luzius, CKD, Mutschler Kitchens of Cleveland, 10523 Carnegie Av., Cleveland, 44106

R. O. Click, CKD, G. Shiekh, CKD, D. Wallace, CKD, Cleveland Tile & Cabinet Co., 131 Terminal Tower Arcade, Cleveland, 44113

J. H. Foster, Jr., CKD, Higbee's Design Center, 100 Public Square, Cleveland, 44113

P. J. Orobello, CKD, A. C. Zigerelli, CKD, National Heating & Plumbing, 3962 Mayfield Road, Cleveland Heights, 44121

J. F. Fehn, CKD, Scioto Kitchen Sales, Inc., 3232 Allegheny Avenue, Columbus, 43209

W. A. Hagedorn, CKD, H & C Kitchens & Bathrooms, Inc., 1290 West Broad Street, Columbus, 43222

J. A. Jacobs, CKD, T. W. Salt, CKD, JAE Company, 955 W. Fifth Avenue, Columbus, 43212

A. J. Boczonadi, CKD, Better Kitchen Supply, 3333 Dayton Zenia Rd., Dayton, 45432

F. A. Lasorella, CKD, Lakeland Building & Construction Co., 36600 Lakeland Blvd., Eastlake, 44094

R. P. Campbell, CKD, A. R. Lingler, CKD, Roth U. Bertsch & Co., Inc., 118 Main Street, Hamilton, 45013

A. R. Driskell, CKD, Tappan Co., Tappan Park, Mansfield, 44901

O. H. Hoge, CKD, Hoge Lumber Co., South Main Street, New Knoxville, 45871

H. J. Harris, CKD, C. F. Bauer Lumber Co., 4575 Hudson Dr., Stow, 44224

J. B. Knowlton, CKD, The Morgan Company, 5400 Oakhill Drive N.W., Warren, 44481

Oregon

V. R. Greb, CKD, J. Greb & Son, Inc., 5027 N.E. 42nd Avenue, Portland, 97218

Pennsylvania

R. Wieland, CKD, Kitchens by Wieland, 4210 Tilghman Street, Allentown, 18104

J. D'Emidio, CKD, F. Licause, CKD, Cameo Kitchens Inc., 2nd Av. & Rte. 13, Bristol, 19007

M. F. Weiss, Jr., CKD, M. F. Weiss, Inc., P.O. Box 97, Brodheadsville, 18322

R. M. Carlson, CKD, Madsen, Inc., 2901 Springfield Road, Broomall, 19008

H. B. Gibb Jr., CKD, Carlisle Kitchen Center, 1034 Harrisburg Pike, Carlisle, 17013

J. H. Stefanide, CKD, Chester Woodworking, Inc., 503 E. 7th Street, Chester, 19013

D. R. Oberholtzer, CKD, R. R. Oberholtzer, CKD, R. G. Snyder, CKD, Oberholtzer Kitchens, Inc., Route 309, Coopersburg, 18036

G. M. Nicolaisen, CKD, Kapri Kitchens, Inc., Div. of Cordal, Corner of Broad & Park St., P. O. Box 100, Dallastown, 17313

J. F. Glunt, CKD, Aaron Kitchen Design Center, 1603 3rd Avenue, Duncansville, 16635

J. J. Dagenhardt, CKD, Gettysburg Building Supply Co., 225 S. Franklin St., Gettysburg, 17325

W. Z. Peterson, CKD, Peterson Cabinet & Supply, 503 New Alexandria Road, Greensburg, 15601

R. M. Fromme, CKD, D & H Distributing Co., 2525 N. 7th Street, Harrisburg, 17105

U. L. Tomassone, CKD, Vogel-Thomas, 713 West Chester Pike, Havertown, 19083

R. L. Selder, CKD, Selders Cabinet Shop, R-784 Cooper Avenue Johnstown, 15906

P. J. Formica, CKD, Formica Cabinet Co., 734 Railroad St., Johnstown, 15902

H. A. Montgomery, CKD, 202 Rear North McKean St., Kittanning, 16201

C. K. Battram Jr., CKD, G. R. Callender, CKD, C. H. Lemmerman, CKD, Wood-Mode Kitchens, Kreamer, 17833

H. P. Dries, CKD, D. J. Bubba, CKD, P. A. Hoffman Jr., CKD, Dries Building Supply Co. Rte. 2 Box 44 Brookside Rd., Macungie, 18062

R. A. Knarr, CKD, Knarr's Kitchen Design Center, Turnpike St., Box 347, Milesburg, 16853

G. D. Lucci Jr., CKD, M. A. Lucci, CKD, R. J. Lucci, CKD, Lucci Kitchens, Inc., 1271 North Brodhead Road, Monaca, 15061

J. W. Brady, CKD, J. W. Brady, Inc., 723 Montgomery Avenue, Narberth, 19072

T. Lamont, CKD, Lamont House of Kitchens, 1990 W. Main Street, Norristown, 19401

D. C. Broscious, CKD, Broscious Lumber Company, 4th & Duke Street, Northumberland, 17857

L. G. Ciliberti, CKD, Sam Donze Kitchens, Inc., 1834-36 E. Passyunk Avenue, Philadelphia, 19148

B. Fleet, CKD, S. Kulla, CKD, J. B. Wagner, CKD, Mayfair Kitchen Remodeling Center, Inc., 7400 Frankford Avenue, Philadelphia, 19136

T. R. Moser, CKD, Moser Corporation, 5702 N. 5th Street, Philadelphia, 19120

L. Raider, CKD, Raider Associates Inc., 843 Disston St., Philadelphia 19111

F. R. Boyd, CKD, Style-Rite Kitchens, 12248 Frankstown Road, Pittsburgh, 15235

L. J. Frey, CKD, Frey Cabinet co., 510 S. Main Street, Pittsburgh, 15220

W. J. Glivic, CKD, Matter Bros., 484 Castle Shannon Blvd., Pittsburgh, 15234

J. J. Molek, CKD, R. Morra, CKD, Morr-Craft Products, Inc., 1414 Spring Garden Avenue, Pittsburgh, 15212

C. P. Morrison, CKD, 4871 Clairton Blvd, Pittsburgh, 15236

G. R. Scull, CKD, Kitchen Sales, Inc., 622 Washington Road, Pittsburgh, 15228

S. Z. Stein, CKD, Steins Custom Interiors, 3559 Bigelow Blvd., Pittsburgh, 15213

W. L. Rotenberger, CKD, Rotenberger Kitchens, 449 Milford Square Rd., Quakertown, 18951

J. G. Heffleger, CKD, J & J Heffleger Custom Kitchens, R. D. #5, Reading, 19605

C. H. Miller, CKD, Kitchen Center of Sharon, 3005 E. State St., Sharon, 16146

A. L. Donze, CKD, S. J. Donze, CKD, Sam Donze Kitchens, Inc., 502 Baltimore Pike, Springfield, 19064

C. J. Walsh, CKD, Wall & Walsh, Inc., 8320 West Chester Pike, Upper Darby, 19082

L. A. Scarf, CKD, Rich Maid Kitchens, Penn Avenue, Wernersville, 19565

H. R. Hurlbrink, CKD, Hurlbrink House of Kitchens, 701 Westtown Road, West Chester, 19380

C. E. Muhly, III, CKD, Conrad E. Muhly Co., 5 Westtown Road, West Chester, 19380

L. Platsky, CKD, M. L. Weisberger, CKD, Betterhouse, Inc., 1140 Wyoming Avenue, Wyoming, 18644

R. D. Botterbusch Jr., CKD, Robert's Kitchens, 790 Carlisle Avenue, York, 17404

H. B. Murray, CKD, Murray Equipment Co., Inc., 1228 E. Philadelphia Street, York, 17405

Rhode Island

J. A. McClure, CKD, American Custom Kitchens, Inc., 145 Chad Brown Street, Providence, 02907

South Carolina

J. A. Clarkson, CKD, Clarkson Kitchen, 946 Harden Street, Columbia, 29205

Tennessee

J. H. Lady, CKD, John Beretta Tile Co. Inc., 217 Walnut St., Knoxville, 37902

M. L. Robinson, CKD, Modern Supply Company, Western Avenue at Dale, Knoxville, 37921

J. R. Henry, CKD, Henry Kitchens, Inc., 1808 Broadway, Nashville, 37203

W. B. Pybas, CKD, Hermitage Electric Supply Corp., 531 Lafayette St., Nashville, 37210

Texas

G. H. Gerdes Jr., CKD, J. B. Lauer, CKD, St. Charles Kitchens of Houston, 2221 Pease, Houston, 77045

D. B. Steffan, CKD, Wood-Mode Kitchens, 2627 Westheimer, Houston, 77006

Utah

K. L. Cowan, CKD, Craftsman Cabinets, 2200 South Main, Salt Lake City, 84115

G. N. Sheffield, CKD, Craftsman Cabinets, Inc., 2200 S. Main Street, Salt Lake City, 84115

Vermont

P. W. Meacham Sr., CKD, Meacham Custom Kitchens, 129 South Crest Dr., Burlington, 05401

P. L. Hackel, CKD, Vermont Electric Supply Co., Inc., 299 N. Main Street, Rutland, 05701

Virginia

R. F. Bartholomew Sr., CKD, Deavers Appliances & Kitchens, 7960 Columbia Pike, Annandale, 22003

M. L. Coll-Pardo, CKD, Lansburgh Contracting Co., 2828 Wilson Blvd., Arlington, 22201

W. A. Dembo Sr., CKD, Kitchen Classics, Inc., 6023 Wilson Blvd., Arlington, 22205

West Virginia

C. H. Coles, CKD, Save Supply Co., Inc., 514 Virginia Street East, Charleston, 25321

Wisconsin

G. F. Soik, CKD, W. Thomas, CKD, Green Bay Kitchen Mart, Inc., 2680 So. Ashland Avenue, Green Bay, 54303

L. C. Thomas, CKD, St. Charles Kitchens by Findorff, 601 W. Wilson St., Madison, 53701

A. B. Mather, CKD, A. Mather Co., 1002 Indiana Avenue, Sheboygan, 53081

Canada

G. A. Dreger, CKD, L. D. Dreger, CKD, K. D. Dreger, CKD, Dreger's Kitchen Corner Ltd., 10442 82 Av., Edmonton, Alberta

K. Cassin, CKD, R. L. Bannerman, CKD, Cassin-Remco Ltd., Box 641, Lambeth, Ontario

G. M. Riepert, CKD, Creative Kitchens, Suite 10, 648A Yonge St., Tornoto, Ontario

Note: Additional kitchen designers are certified each month. For the newest listings in your area, write AIKD, 114 Main St., Hackettstown, N.J. 07840.

Index